out
AROUND

Paris

out
AROUND

Paris

By Tim Mowbray

Thomas Cook Publishing

The Pink Paper

Published by Thomas Cook Publishing
PO Box 227
The Thomas Cook Business Park
Coningsby Road
Peterborough
PE3 8XX

Email: books@thomascook.com

ISBN: 1841571 598

For Thomas Cook Publishing
Managing Director: Kevin Fitzgerald
Publisher: Donald Greig
Commissioning Editor: Deborah Parker
Editors: Sarah Hudson, Helen Partington
Proofreader: Anne O'Rorke

For Pink Paper
General Manager: David Bridle
Publishing Manager: Mike Ross
Editor: Steve Anthony
Additional picture research: Claire Benjamin

Design: Studio 183 and Grassverge
Layout: Studio 183, Peterborough
Cover Design: Studio 183 and Grassverge
Cover Artwork: Steve Clarke, Studio 183

City maps drawn by: Steve Munns
Transport maps: Transport Cartographic Service

Scanning: Dale Carrington, Chronos Publishing; David Bruce Graphics

Printed and bound in Spain by: Artes Gráficas Elkar, Loiu, Spain

Written and researched by Tim Mowbray

Photography: Gavin Harrison

Additional photography: Denise O'Brien, pages 67, 70, 82, 93, 98, 100 (Thermik), 109, 116 and 120.

The following are thanked for supplying photographs, to whom the copyright belongs:
Mike and Edith Summerhayes (page 46)
Walt Disney Corporation 113, 114

Contents

CONTENTS

Prices throughout this book are given in Francs as many of their euro values had not been finalised at the time of going to press.

1 € = 6.56 F

My Kind of Town...

With its bright, modern bars, classical buildings and rich cultural life, Paris is one of the hottest destinations for the gay traveller. Whether you're looking for great clubs and bars, the best in sightseeing, museums or some tasty French cuisine, it's all here.

Having spent much of my writing career trawling gay bars, clubs and the arts scene in London, Paris was a dream-ticket destination. Exploring its *joie de vivre* is easy due to its compact, easily walkable size. The 'A Day Out' sections in this guide should help you familiarise yourself with the city quickly and painlessly.

For the first-time visitor, all the famous sights and museums are included, providing a backdrop to the city's historical, social and cultural life, with things of particular interest to the gay traveller and off-beat attractions highlighted to give a pinker peek at Parisian life. Of course, any book on Gay Paree wouldn't be complete without information on the hippest bars, clubs and shops. Whether you want to stay in a gay-owned hotel or eat at a restaurant with queer cuisine, you've come to the right place.

Tim Mowbray wishes to thank: Paul Burston, who got me started; Mike Ross who put me onto this project; Deborah Parker, who saw it through; and my flat mates, who put up with me while I was writing it! He would also like to thank all at the Hotel Central, Eurostar and everyone who pointed me in the right direction in Paris and the UK.

Signage with style

Out in Paris

Ah Paris! The 'city of lights'. The clichés come fast and furious when describing the French capital, and all for good reason. Admired for its romance, history and innovative fashion design, Paris is the picture postcard that delivers. Everywhere you look, the city comes alive with the songs and stories that are embedded in the hearts and minds of people the world over. From Victor Hugo's *Hunchback of Nôtre-Dame* to Edith Piaf's *La Vie en Rose*, Paris remains a city of contrasts; of fairytale magic and real-life struggle overtaken by the demands of the modern world.

If you're out and proud, Paris is also one of the most liberal of Europe's major cities. This is exemplified within the Marais, where gay couples walk hand-in-hand and many of the bars proudly display the universal rainbow flag as a welcoming symbol. The narrow streets of Le Marais are also home to some of the city's most beautiful architecture and museums, which transformed this former swamp into one of Paris's essential places to visit.

Beyond the Marais, the nearby district of Les Halles has also been 'gay gentrified', its bustling streets often overtaking the Marais for sheer boisterousness. Outside these central *quartiers*, the signs of gay freedom are less obvious but Parisians generally believe sexuality to be a private matter and violent crimes against gay men are rare.

The advent of François Mitterrand's presidency in the 1990s saw the age of consent lowered to 15 and homophobic statutes revoked. However, the AIDS (SIDA) epidemic propagated a less tolerant attitude towards gay men, forcing gay Parisians to become more politically active.

Just as the Marais has led the way in hedonism and hotpants, the Bastille's traditionally revolutionary streets have become the focal point for gay political movements, with the Gay and Lesbian Centre and Act-Up Paris based here. Even the boys from the Marais, usually content with partying the night away, fought back when heavy-handed police using dodgy licensing laws closed down some of the bars in the area.

This show of people power should surprise no one familiar with Paris's rebellious history. Back in the 1340s, a series of revolts around the time of the Black Death saw everyone from the bourgeoisie to the peasants kicking up their heels. The storming of the Bastille prison in 1789 marked the continuation of the French Revolutionary tradition, and subsequent riots by workers and students brought the city to a halt in 1830 and 1968 respectively. Today, workers' rights

Glitzy nightlife

remain a major cause of industrial action in Paris, although violence is rarely involved. If you're unlucky enough to visit the city when the public transport workers are on strike, you're unlikely to encounter any bemoaning of the workers: Parisians usually save their grievances for those higher up the food chain.

Recent swaying of political favour towards the left is also likely to support freedom for the people to strike and improve minority relations. The arrival of a new gay socialist mayor, Bertrand Delanoe, in 2001 sent encouraging signals throughout the gay community and the social scene is more ebullient than ever. Shortly after his landmark victory, Delanoe made a speech in which he outlined the 'values of Paris' as 'Human rights, freedom, fraternity and cultural diversity.' The PAX bill, introduced in 2000, provided gay couples with a legally binding 'marriage' ceremony, including all the rights associated with heterosexual partnerships. On ground level, however, Paris remains a city of vastly differing opinions and attitudes. Many of the more traditional pockets of the city remain far removed from the Marais lifestyle and bearing this in mind will make your visit far more enjoyable.

This, however, doesn't mean that the French are generally an unfriendly nation – far from it. Learning to say 'please' and 'thank you' (in French) before you arrive will mean that you are much more likely to be well received. But it is also useful to remember that any large city is populated by the polite and impolite, so don't take out your annoyance with one on the other. Slamming your money on the bar and demanding a drink won't make you any friends, wherever you are. In Paris, you're likely to be ignored!

In addition to its wealth of sightseeing (and photo) opportunities, the city also has a lot of gay cultural attractions on offer. The many free gay publications, available in bars and cafés such as *em@le* and *illico*, include features

Glam Metro entrance

on arts, politics and entertainment, in addition to club and bar listings. A fairly recent addition to the gay paid-for magazine stable is *Têtu*, with its bright, sexy covers and knowing features on everything from politics to pop music.

Parisian history is littered with gay icons from Edith Piaf to Oscar Wilde, both of whom are buried at the famous Père Lachaise cemetery

Gay Paree

only a short Métro ride from the city centre. Edmund White, author of *A Boy's Own Story* (1982), also lived here for many years and Cyril Collard communicated the darker side of a city overtaken by AIDS in his semi-autobiographical novel *Savage Nights* (1989).

The sexual freedom transmitted through fiction lives large in modern Paris. Wherever you go, Parisians like to catch your eye and gay men have mastered the art of public flirting. Whether you are sitting in a coffee shop, riding the Métro or walking down the street, there's a good chance you'll come under the admiring gaze of a stranger. In some cities this would be considered too forward; in Paris it seems the most natural thing in the world and a great way of meeting new people.

Even the bars display the kind of relaxed social interaction lost in many cities. as men stop off for a drink with their dog in tow and a copy of *Le Monde* under their arm. During the summer, in late June, when the Gay Pride parade takes place, the men from the Marais make an utterly outrageous dash for their wardrobe, then head for the Bastille and a day of semi-political partying. Slightly later in the year, in July, it's a similar story, this time at the Bastille Day Ball, a wild open-air dance-a-thon on the Quai De La Tournelle just by the river Seine.

Whatever you're looking for in Paris, it's unlikely you'll be short of something to do. On the contrary, the main problem will be deciding what to do next. For gay men, the list is endless.

The symbol of the city

Stepping Out

Looking for something of interest in Paris isn't difficult. Attractions are all around you. With so much on offer, picking recommendations isn't easy. Some, such as the Eiffel Tower and the Louvre, may seem rather obvious, but leaving them out isn't an option – they remain must-see sights. However, I have included something for every taste. From the Edith Piaf Museum to Oscar Wilde's resting place to the mammoth Arc de Triomphe, the biggest and best are all here.

My Top Sights

Eiffel Tower

Champ de Mars, 75007 | 01 44 11 23 45
9.30am–11pm daily | 62F | RER Champ-de-Mars

The symbol of Paris, the Eiffel Tower is often the first sight tourists make a beeline for to say that they've 'arrived'. Standing at over 300m (984 ft) and with around six million visitors annually, the Eiffel Tower, or Tour Eiffel as it is known in France, remains one of Paris's top attractions.

Made from 700 tons of criss-crossed steel, it was designed in 1889 in a competition for the World's Fair Exhibition. It won despite stiff competition from over 700 other entries. Originally regarded by locals as a monstrous blight on the Parisian landscape, most Parisians wouldn't part with the large phallic symbol now emblazoned on almost every piece of tourist tat for sale within the city's borders.

Writer Emile Zola and Charles Garnier, designer of the Opéra-Garnier, both wanted the tower scrapped and their cries were almost heeded. In 1909, when its planning permission expired, the tower was on the point of being torn down in a blaze of publicity, surviving only due to its importance as a mast for the newly created radio service.

During the 1980s, an ambitious restoration programme got underway. The tower was strengthened and 1,340 tons of unnecessary material removed. In 1986, the tower's night-time floodlights were replaced by a state-of-the-art illumination system, attracting an influx of new visitors. But it's the view from the top of the tower that remains a big draw for visitors and Parisians alike. (*See p. 47.*)

Arc de Triomphe

place Charles de Gaulle, 75008 | 01 43 80 31 31 | daily 9.30am–11pm (Apr–Oct); 10am–10.30pm (Nov–Mar) | Charles de Gaulle-Etoile

Napoleonic arch

Conceived by Napoleon in 1806 to honour his military forces and further stamp his seal on the city's architecture, the Arc de Triomphe provides impeccable views of Paris's *pièce de résistance*, the Champs-Elysées and the 12 avenues that form a star from the centre of the place de l'Etoile. Intricately carved with 30 shields and the names of 30 Napoleonic victories, the Arc remains a powerful symbol of battles fought, won and lost. Underneath lies the Tomb of the Unknown Soldier, who died in World War I. Each year, a Remembrance Day service is held here to commemorate the lighting of the Eternal Flame on 11 November. Ironically, on 14 July each year, Bastille Day sees the President head down the Champs-Elysées flanked by tanks, guns and flags to commemorate the French Revolution. (*See p. 52.*)

Victor Hugo's House

6 place des Vosges, 75004
01 42 72 10 16
Tue–Sun 10am–5.40pm
Shop accepts MasterCard, Visa
St-Paul

Place des Vosges

Victor Hugo, the author of *The Hunchback of Nôtre-Dame* and *Les Misérables* (1862), lived in this house until 1848, when his political views forced him to flee the country. He eventually settled on the island of Guernsey with his wife and children. This three-storey museum is a constant reminder to Parisians of one of their greatest literary talents. Along with portraits, manuscripts and other memorabilia is a specially designed Japanese dining room created for his lover's house, as well as a good collection of photographs and other artwork by the author. Pictures of his family during their 15-year exile in Guernsey and the desk where Hugo wrote his world-famous classics highlight both his public and private persona. (*See p. 22.*)

Pompidou Centre

rue Beaubourg, 75004
01 44 78 12 33
Mon, Wed–Fri 12noon–10pm; Sat, Sun 10am–10pm
Shop accepts MasterCard, Visa, American Express Hôtel-de-Ville

Ultra-modern on the outside and filled with the some of the most celebrated contemporary art, the Pompidou Centre has become as much a part of Paris as the Eiffel Tower. Comprising a number of garishly coloured pipes attached to a steel infrastructure, the building

Inside-out architecture

was considered an eyesore on completion in 1977. Originally intended only as a temporary structure, the Pompidou was designed by British architect Richard Rogers. The pipes on the outside of the building provide Beaubourg (as it is known in Paris) with electricity, water and other essential supplies in a brilliant synthesis of form and function. Inside is Paris's largest library, incorporating every modern-day technological gadget. The National Museum of Modern Art is also based here, along with temporary exhibitions. The sixth floor has a truly panoramic view of Paris. (*See p. 22.*)

Oscar's tomb

Père-Lachaise Cemetery

boulevard de Ménilmontant, 75020
01 55 25 82 10
daily 9am–5.30pm.
Père Lachaise

Looking like a miniature city of its own, Père-Lachaise is where the who's who of Paris's past and present eventually wind up. Jim Morrison of The Doors rests his head here, watched over by the vandalism police, along with neighbours Sarah Bernhard, Marcel Proust and the composer Chopin. For the gay visitor, Oscar Wilde remains one of the cemetery's biggest draws, his tomb inscribed with a verse from 'The Ballad of Reading Gaol' and watched over by Jacob Epstein's sculpture of a winged messenger.

The north end of the cemetery is where *chanteuse* Edith Piaf is buried in a family grave. The nearby Edith Piaf Museum, featuring hundreds of her personal belongings, has become a popular attraction for older gay fans captivated by her dramatic struggles with life and her reputed affair with legendary *chanteuse* and fellow star, Marlene Dietrich. (*See p. 34.*)

The basilica

Sacré-Coeur

35 rue de Chevalier, 75018
01 53 41 89 00
Open daily 9am–6pm
Crypt/Dome 30F
Abbesses

Crowning the Butte Montmartre, the Sacré-Coeur – with its whitewashed domes and mis-matched architecture – is not considered to be one of Paris's most beautiful basilicas; however, it still offers some great views of the city. If you're feeling energetic you can walk up through place Willette, or take the *funiculaire* (cable car). Construction began in the 1870s, driven by the Catholic Church's desire to atone for lives lost during the Franco-Prussian War, but completion didn't arrive until 1914 due to the death of its architect, Paul Abadie.

The basilica looks out at the surrounding area of Montmartre, which made its name during the postwar period as the showcase for up-and-coming young artists. The after-effects of this cultural explosion are still visible today, evidenced by the numerous canvasses (some of rather dubious quality) that dot the neighbourhood's winding streets. (*See p. 59.*)

Nôtre-Dame

place du Parvis-Nôtre Dame, 75004
01 42 34 56 10
Mon–Fri 8am–6.45pm; Sat–Sun 8am–7.45pm
Admission free; towers 35F
Cité/RER St Michel

The inspiration for Victor Hugo's novel *The Hunchback of Nôtre-Dame* of 1831, La Cathédrale de Nôtre-Dame has a history like no other in Paris. Mary Queen of Scots' coronation was held here and Joan of Arc, a reputed lesbian, was condemned to death within its sturdy walls.

Completed in 1345, almost 200 years after its conception, the cathedral's stunning gothic architecture is at once recognisable from its crocketed gables and intricately carved steeples. From across the Seine, its fairytale appearance offers an array of photo opportunities, as does its rooftop, from which you get a stunning view of the surrounding area.

The 13-ton Emmanuel Bell hangs in the South Tower. From the North Tower the infamous gargoyles, added during renovation work in the 19th century can be seen. (*See p. 61.*)

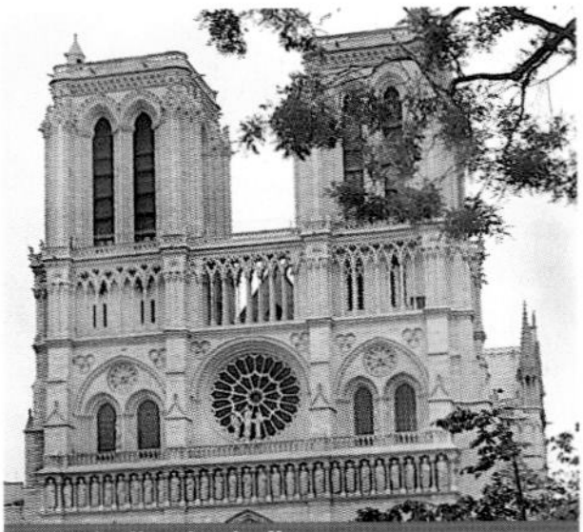

The bells, the bells . . .

Ancient and modern

Louvre

The route to Art

Entrance through Carrousel du Louvre shopping centre or through the Pyramid on ground level, 99 rue de Rivoli, 75001

01 40 20 50 50

Mon, Thur–Sun 9am–6pm, Wed 9am–9.45pm

46F until 3pm, 30F after 3pm, free to under 18s first Sun of month; temporary exhibitions 25F; Mastercard, Visa

Louvre-Rivoli

Beautifully located near the Tuileries Gardens and the Seine, the Louvre is blessed with a world-renowned art collection. The *Mona Lisa* is here, as is Da Vinci's *Venus de Milo*. Divided into three wings, the museum has over 400,000 items spread throughout 200 rooms.

Originally built in 1200 as a fortress to defend the city, it first opened to the public during the Revolution in 1793. When Mitterrand became President in 1981 he commissioned the giant glass pyramid designed by I. M. Pei to replace the original entrance. Queues can stretch for hours, so visit early in the day if possible. (*See p. 28.*)

The stunning Pompidou Centre

Around Town

You'll probably want to get to the heart of the city in a matter of days, so I have focused on those areas with the highest concentration of sights and attractions, particularly for the gay visitor. Outlying areas of the city have mostly been omitted, not because they have nothing to offer but because they have less to offer those on a brief or first-time visit. Gay life and style flourishes in the Marais, the Bastille and Les Halles.

The Marais and Beaubourg

The heart of gay Paris, the Marais represents just how far the city has come in terms of acceptance of gay people. Here, the old sits comfortably alongside the new. The Jewish Quarter around the rue de Rosiers, with its kosher delis and specialist food shops, tempts the taste buds by day. At night, the gay bars and boulevards in and around the rue Vieille-du-Temple can't fail to catch your eye, as gay men from across the city gravitate towards the temptations that await. Once a swamp, the Marais was transformed in 1605 by Henri IV, whose place des Vosges kick-started a building boom that regenerated the area. To the west, the Pompidou Centre exhibits the best in contemporary art, while in the place des Vosges, Victor Hugo's house, now a museum, reveals the man behind the novels *Les Misérables* and *The Hunchback of Nôtre-Dame*. Museums, bars and succulent suppering holes remain at the heart of the Marais, providing something for every taste.

A DAY OUT

The Pompidou Centre (*see p. 15*) is a relatively recent addition to Paris, having only been open since 1977. Today, the Pompidou is Paris's most visited attraction, outdoing even the Eiffel Tower and the Louvre. Follow the signposts or follow the crowds from Rambuteau Métro station to find it. Considered ugly by many Parisians, its garish tubular outer casing hides a series of wide-open spaces and some of the best contemporary art from around the world. Buy a ticket before heading up to level 4 to

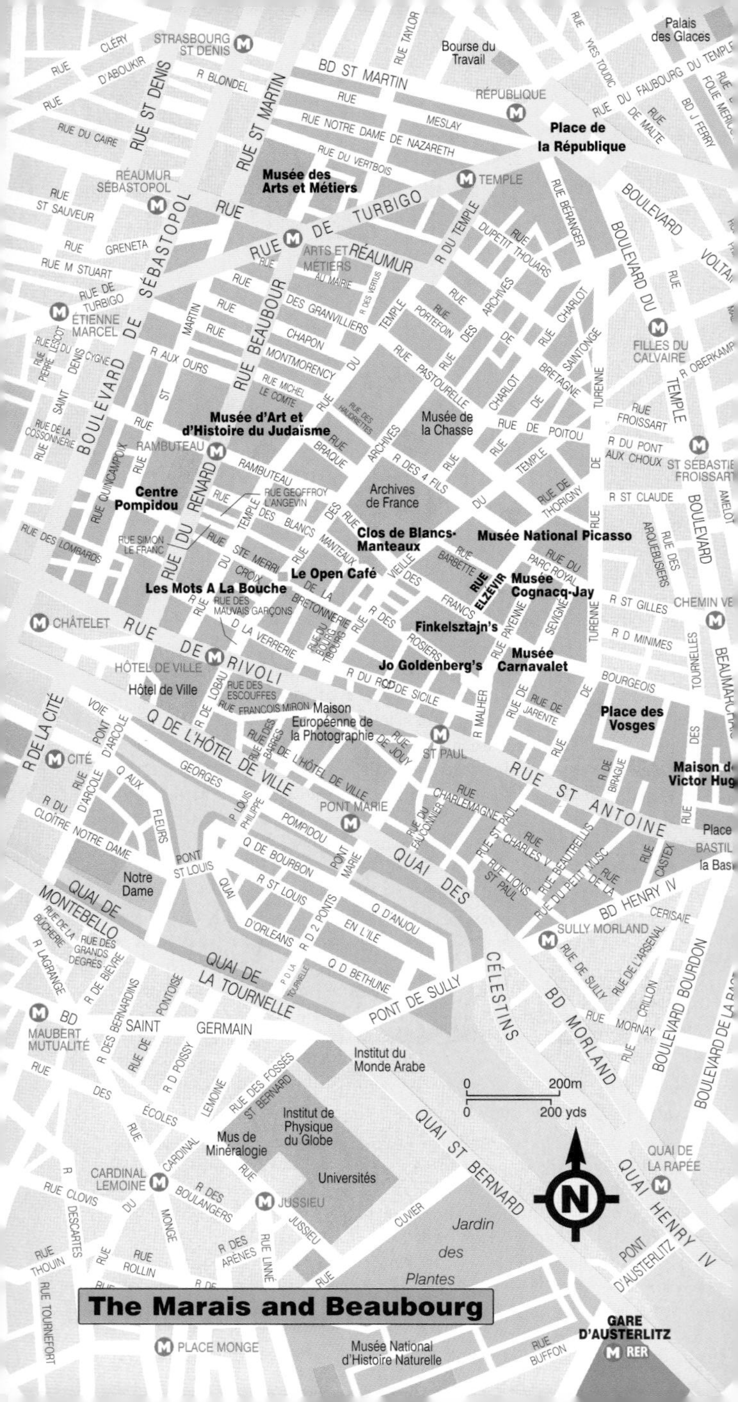

The Marais and Beaubourg

catch the art world's hottest new names and the best in pop art. On your way up – if you take the escalators – the view becomes gradually more spectacular the higher you go. On the fifth floor, 'Modern Origins' includes work by Picasso and Matisse, with the top floor featuring hip restaurant George's (*see p. 22*) and some of the best views of Paris. Leaving the busy Pompidou Centre behind, make your way to the back of the building, crossing into the rue St-Merri. This will take you into the heart of the Marais. On the corner of rue des Archives is Le Open Café (see Out to Lunch feature), one of the neighbourhood's most popular gay café/bars. Outside seating makes it the perfect place to stop for coffee.

The busy rue Ste-Croix-de-la-Bretonnerie features some of the *quartier's* most popular gay fashion outlets, with gay bookstore Le Mots à La Bouche located at number 6 (*see p. 70*). South of here is the rue des Rosiers, known as the Jewish Quarter and worth exploring for its kosher delis, bread and cheese shops. Finkelsztajn's delicatessen, at number 27, has some of the finest kosher food and aromas to match. At number 7 is Jo Goldenberg's restaurant (*see p. 83*), popular with authentic Jewish food lovers and bombed by far-right terrorists in the 1980s.

Despite being just moments away from the busy rue de Rivoli, the Jewish Quarter remains a peaceful place to soak up the sights and sounds of the Marais. Head east to the Musée Picasso, where in addition to seeing work from all phases of Picasso's career, you can admire one of the city's most beautiful mansions. In the place des Vosges, on the edge of the Marais, stands the Maison de Victor Hugo. The author of the infamous *Hunchback of Nôtre-Dame* lived at number 6 until 1848 when his political beliefs came into conflict with ruler Napoleon III, forcing the author to flee the country. Hugo's personal belongings, from letters and journals to the desk where he worked, are all here, including many photographs of his wife and family. Climb the large wooden staircase where the man himself once walked for views of the place des Vosges from the second-floor windows.

Out to Lunch

The Marais can be both a stimulating and a relaxing place to eat and watch the world go by. Café culture has really taken hold here, with everything on offer from à-la-carte cuisine to tasty basics. Why not stop off at **Le Open Café** (*see p. 82*) for coffee and a sandwich for around 55F, or try **L'Open Coffee Shop** (*see p. 84*), only a few doors away, for something more substantial from around 150F. **Coffee Shop Central** (*see p. 83*), near the famous cruising corner of rue-Vieille-du-Temple and rue Ste-Croix-de-la-Bretonnerie, is also a good choice for light meals for around 50F. Stop off next door at **Boys' Bazaar** if you like shopping while you snack (*see p. 67*).

OUTLINES

CENTRE POMPIDOU

rue Beaubourg, 75004
01 44 78 12 33
Mon, Wed–Fri noon–10pm; Sat, Sun 10am–10pm
Shop accepts MasterCard, Visa, American Express
Hôtel-de-Ville

The architecture might not be to everybody's taste, but this massive arts complex houses the biggest library in Paris in addition to a fantastic collection of visiting and permanent art collections. George's, on the sixth floor, offers up-to-the-minute dishes and fantastic views (see sightseeing recommendations, p. 15).

Old and modern side by side

CLOS DE BLANCS-MANTEAUX

21 rue des Blancs-Manteaux, 75003
01 42 28 47 63
Sat, Sun 10am–5pm

Unveiled on Valentine's Day by ex-Mayor of Paris Jean Tiberi, this small but compact garden features 250 species of plants chosen for their ecological, symbolic, culinary or medicinal worth. The geometrical beds are said to have been inspired by the Marais' historic walled gardens.

MAISON DE VICTOR HUGO

6 place des Vosges, 75004
01 42 72 10 16
Tue–Sun 10am–5.40pm
Shop accepts MasterCard, Visa
St-Paul

The famous author of the *Hunchback of Nôtre-Dame* and *Les Misérables* lived in this town house until Napoleon forced him out of Paris (see sightseeing recommendations, p. 14).

MUSÉE D'ART ET D'HISTOIRE DU JUDAISME

Hôtel de St-Aignan, 71 rue du Temple, 75003
01 42 57 84 15
Mon–Fri 11am–6pm, Sun 10am–6pm;
40F; 25F under 26s; free under 18s
Shop accepts MasterCard, Visa
Arts et Métiers

Another Marais mansion turned museum, this time providing a unique insight into Jewish heritage. Exhibits include work by Modigliani, Chagall and Soutine.

MUSÉE DES ARTS ET MÉTIERS

60 rue Réaumur, 75003
01 53 01 82 00
Tue, Wed, Fri, Sun 10am–6pm; Thur 10am–9.30pm
MasterCard, Visa, American Express

Science and technology are the focus

of this newly re-opened museum, which features Foucault's pendulum, a Blériot monoplane and Bartholdi's study for the Statue of Liberty. Situated in a medieval abbey, the museum's collection has more than 80,000 machines and models, with interactive video screens and gadgets doing much to explain their scientific origins. Follow the steel and glass staircase up to the nave for a close-up view of the suspended models.

MUSÉE CARNAVALET

23 rue de Sévigné, 75003
01 44 59 58 58
Tue–Sun 10am–5.40pm
30F, visiting exhibitions 20F; under 26 15F with ID. Shop accepts MasterCard, Visa, American Express
Saint-Paul

The history of Paris unfolds with exhibits through the ages, including sculptures,

Musée Carnavalet

paintings, furniture and drawings. Originally used to house interiors from demolished buildings during redevelopment programmes in the city from 1866, the museum displays everything in chronological order, making it easy to see how styles have evolved. There are entire rooms devoted to French literature and you can even see a chunk of the Bastille prison after it was levelled. From Napoleon's cradle to Proust's bedroom, it's pretty much all here.

MUSÉE COGNACQ-JAY

8 rue Elzévir, 75003
01 40 27 07 21
Tue–Sun 10am–5.40pm
Saint-Paul

A grand collection of 18th-century art started by the founder of the Samaritaine department store and his wife. Displayed in the 16th-century Hôtel Donon, the museum includes paintings by Gainsborough, Canaletto and Rembrandt in addition to an impressive collection of furniture, jewellery and sculpture. Much of the collection is French, with work

A collection of art

from the 18th century dominating. English, Dutch and Flemish pieces are also displayed.

MUSÉE NATIONAL PICASSO

5 rue de Thorigny, 75003
01 42 71 25 21
Mon, Wed–Sun 9.30am–5.30pm
Shop accepts MasterCard, Visa, American Express
Chemin-Vert

This grand Marais mansion houses some of Picasso's best work from every period of his career, including his Cubist and classical phases. Portraits of some of his favourite models, including Dora Marr and Marie-Thérèse, are worthy of note, contrasting as they do with earlier works like his self-portrait, *Paolo as Harlequin,* and his collection of tribal art. Paintings by Matisse, Rousseau and other contemporaries provide a contrast to the master's own work.

Coffee with a smile

Les Halles and the Louvre

Bustling and crammed with tourists, yet still exciting and glamorous, Les Halles is at the heart of modern Paris and just a few minutes away from the gay quarter, the Marais. Once a market district, its redevelopment saw the market move to the suburbs in 1969, turning what was once a working-class area into a popular place for shopping and partying. Many gay bars and clubs have popped up along the route between the Marais and Châtelet-les-Halles. A rainbow flag fluttering above many a door welcomes visitors from around the world. Along the rue de Rivoli stands the world-famous Louvre museum, with its shimmering glass pyramid and underground Carrousel du Louvre shopping centre, contrasting the historic beauty of the gallery with the stylish modernity of today's Paris.

A DAY OUT

Exploring Les Halles and the Louvre can do much to test your patience at all times of the year. Summer months are always packed, making queues generally unavoidable. For this reason, visiting the Louvre should always be the first stop on your itinerary. Arriving at about 10am will ensure that you prevent any long delays waiting in line. The best way into the Louvre is through the underground passageways that lead from the Métro Louvre, making up the Carrousel du Louvre shopping centre. It also gives you a chance to wander through the maze of fashion chains and smaller, more exclusive stores that comprise the large *centre d'achats*.

Having bought your ticket and picked up a guide of the museum, head for the Denon wing, where Da Vinci's *Mona Lisa* (*La Jaconde*) is housed. Follow the grand staircase up to the ground floor and you will come face to face with the powerful *Venus de Milo*. If you have time, visit the galleries exhibiting French Romantics,

The Pyramid at the Louvre

Les Halles and the Louvre

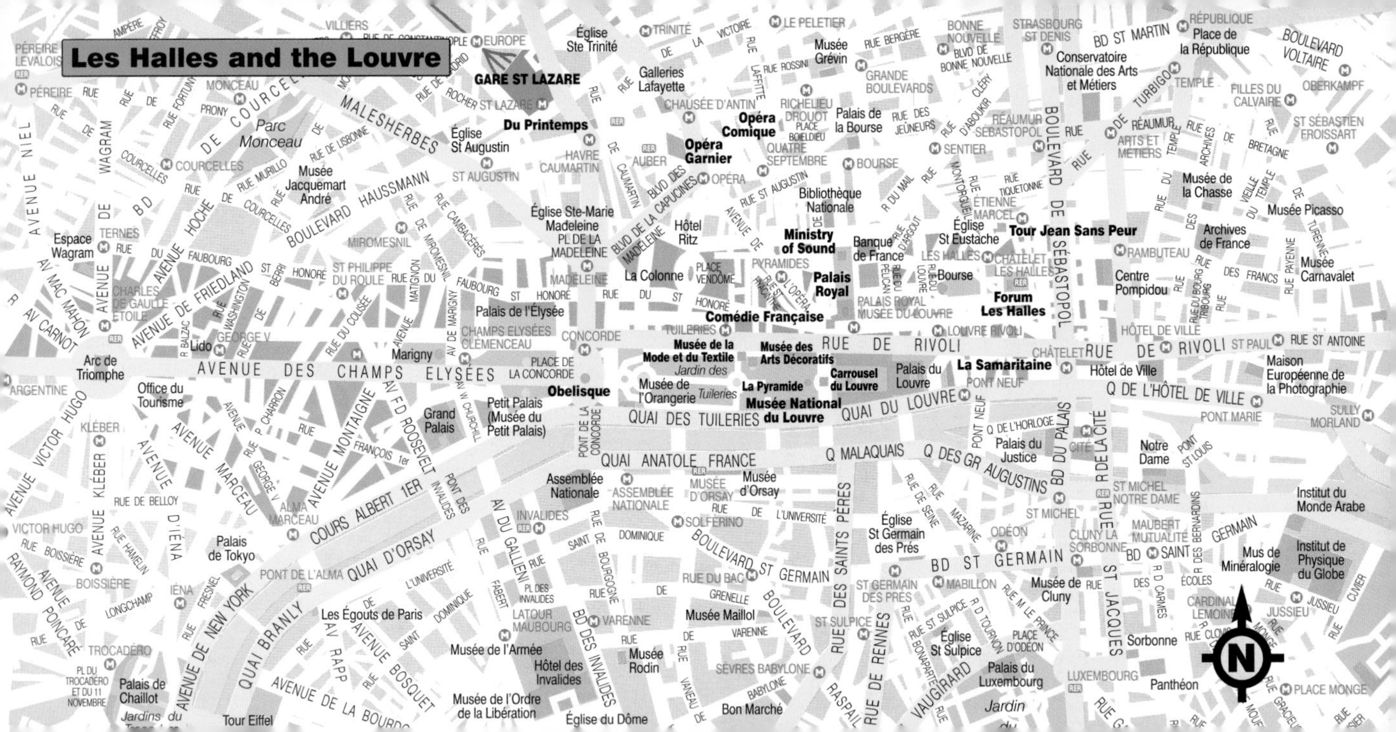

including Delacroix's *Liberty Leading the People*, the Egyptian antiquities, and the collection of Islamic and decorative art.

When you exit the Louvre take time to wander the grand courtyards that surround the Pyramid at ground level. Parallel with the entrance to the Pyramid stands the Arc de Triomphe du Carrousel, completed in 1808 and celebrating Napoleon's 1805 victories at Austerlitz.

Heading west towards place de La Concorde and the Obelisk of Luxor (see the section on the Champs-Elysées *p. 48*) lie the Tuileries gardens, originally created for Catherine de Médicis in the 1570s but redesigned and later used by wealthy Parisians as a place to party and impress friends and acquaintances. Today the gardens are for all Parisians and visitors to enjoy. Two open-air cafés make it the perfect stopping-off point for a coffee and croissant.

The Tuileries have also become a popular cruising spot for gay men, who wander along the tree-lined pathways looking for love. Nearby, the Palais Royal, built in 1630, was once the residence of Cardinal Richelieu. The Ministry of Culture now calls this imposing building home, and even flings the garden gates open for the *hoi polloi* to enjoy.

Just along the rue de Rivoli, adjoining the Louvre, is the Musée des Arts Décoratifs at number 107. Having recently undergone a revamp, this fine museum displays impressive collections of Renaissance tapestries, ivories and Venetian glass, which have boosted the museum's existing marvels of interior design. The gift shop is an especially welcome find, offering a wonderful combination of the best in classic and contemporary design.

Out to Lunch

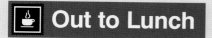

If you're looking for a snack or for something more substantial, Les Halles has it all. The rue de Rivoli has a plethora of brasseries that sell everything from *Le Campagnard* (potatoes and bacon grilled on farmhouse bread) to simple, modestly priced lunches. **The Jardin des Tuileries**, however, is the perfect place to stop for coffee. **La Terrasse de Pomone** is one of two cafés between the entrance to the gardens and the place de la Concorde and serves coffee at around 21F. If you have a penchant for *poisson*, give **L'Atelier Berger**, at 49 rue Berger (01 40 28 00 00), a try or head for **L' Amazonial** (*see p. 81*) on rue Sainte-Opportune for a slice of gay life.

What's on the menu?

OUTLINES

FORUM DES HALLES

1–7 rue Pierre Lesust 75001

Châtelet-Les-Halles

This bustling shopping centre in the heart of Les Halles district looks pretty shabby these days, due at least in part to the accumulation of litter and crime that has become synonymous with the area immediately around it. What it lacks in looks, however, it makes up for in shopping opportunities. Here, you'll find just about every style of clothing, fad and fashion frippery known to man, including many chain stores. Also on offer are a swimming pool, cinema multiplex and plenty of gay bars, including the Banana Café and Le Tropic.

MUSÉE DE LA MODE ET DU TEXTILE

107 rue de Rivoli, 75001

01 44 55 57 50

Tue, Thur, Fri

11am–6pm, Wed 11am–10pm, Sat, Sun 10am–6pm.

Palais-Royal

Palais Royal

Fashion museum housing an enormous vault of more than four centuries of Parisian couture. The exhibition is changed annually, so gay fashion obsessives have the perfect excuse to come back again and again.

MUSÉE DES ARTS DÉCORATIFS

105 rue de Rivoli, 75001

01 44 55 37 50

Tue–Sun 10am–5.30pm; Wed until 9pm; closed some public holidays

35F adults, 25F 18–25s, free under 18s

Mastercard, Visa, American Express

From medieval times through to modern-day Paris, this collection of decorative items remains a must-see for gay design students and glamour queens. Collections of wallpaper, Venetian glass and elaborate furnishings are all being improved upon as part of the Grand Louvre Project, due for completion in early 2003. Until then, there remains plenty to feast your eyes upon, including a Gothic Charles VIII bedchamber and some beautifully reconstructed period rooms.

MUSÉE NATIONAL DU LOUVRE

Entrance through Carrousel du Louvre shopping centre or through the Pyramid on ground level, 99 rue de Rivoli, 75001

01 40 20 50 50

Mon, Thur–Sun 9am–6pm; Wed 9am–9.45pm

46F until 3pm, 30F after 3pm, free to under 18s first Sun of month;

temporary exhibitions 25F
Mastercard, Visa
Louvre-Rivoli

Filled with artistic gems, the Louvre remains one of Paris's most popular attractions. Just about every major artist is here, from Botticelli to Turner, making it a must-see for devout art lovers. The museum also has an interesting collection of Islamic and Oriental art, in addition to its better-known collection of paintings from Italy, Spain, Greece and other European countries. There is also an impressive collection of Egyptian antiquities, including a giant Sphinx made out of pink granite and a room full of mummified cats. If the queues prevent you from going inside, the pyramid entrance is also pretty spectacular, especially viewed after dark.

PALAIS ROYAL

place du Palais-Royal, 75001
Palais-Royal

Formerly the home of Cardinal Richelieu, the Palais was once used to entertain the Parisian elite. Today, it remains closed to the public, leaving only the gardens open to in-the-know Parisians spending a lazy lunch hour. The nearby antiques shops add a cultured feel to the inner-city oasis and artist Daniel Buren's controversial black-and-white striped columns in the front courtyard remain a popular talking point since their inception in 1982.

TOUR JEAN SANS PEUR

20 rue Etienne Marcel, 75002
01 40 26 20 28
Tue–Sun 1.30pm–6pm
30F, 50F guided tour
Etienne-Marcel

This ornate town house was once the home of Jean Sans Peur (literally translated as 'Jean without fear'), Ducs de Bourgogne, whose assassination of Louis d'Orleans kick-started

You are here

the Hundred Years' War. Today, it stands as an impressive example of the architecture of the time. The ornately carved tower, which was added to the mansion when Sans Peur returned to Paris fleeing numerous hired assassins, was his final improvement to the house; they finally got to him in 1419.

Way to the Louvre

The Colonne de Juillet

Bastille and East

When the Bastille prison was stormed on 14 July 1789, the world sat up and took notice. Today, the Opéra Bastille, originally built to be an 'opera of the people', stands in its place. It is not considered a particularly attractive addition to local architecture, but the history of the area and its gradual redevelopment into a trendy place to eat and explore arts and crafts make it worth visiting. As with many parts of the city, the gay bar scene has also begun to get a foothold. The gay and lesbian centre is based nearby in rue Keller and gay designer Jean-Paul Gaultier chose the Bastille for his newest shop. Along the boulevard Richard Lenoir, a local produce market has all the best buys on Thursdays and Sundays, while a short walk east to avenue Daumesnil demonstrates that the area's creative flair remains very much alive. The Musée des Arts d'Afrique et d'Océanie houses a fantastic collection of African Art and an aquarium with live crocodiles and some spectacular fish.

A DAY OUT

The first thing you are likely to notice about place de la Bastille is the traffic. It moves fast and stops for no one, so when crossing the road to take a closer look at the Opéra Bastille, take the subway that runs from the Métro and emerges just outside the opera house.

avenue Daumesnil

Standing in the centre of the busy roundabout is a bronze column, erected to commemorate those Parisians who died in the uprising between 1830 and 1848 and during the storming of the Bastille. Take boulevard Richard Lenoir, where a busy produce market is situated on Thursdays and Sundays, offering up stall after stall of delicious foods from cheeses to seafood. From here, walk along the rue de Lyon to the south of place de la Bastille and turn left on to avenue Daumesnil, where

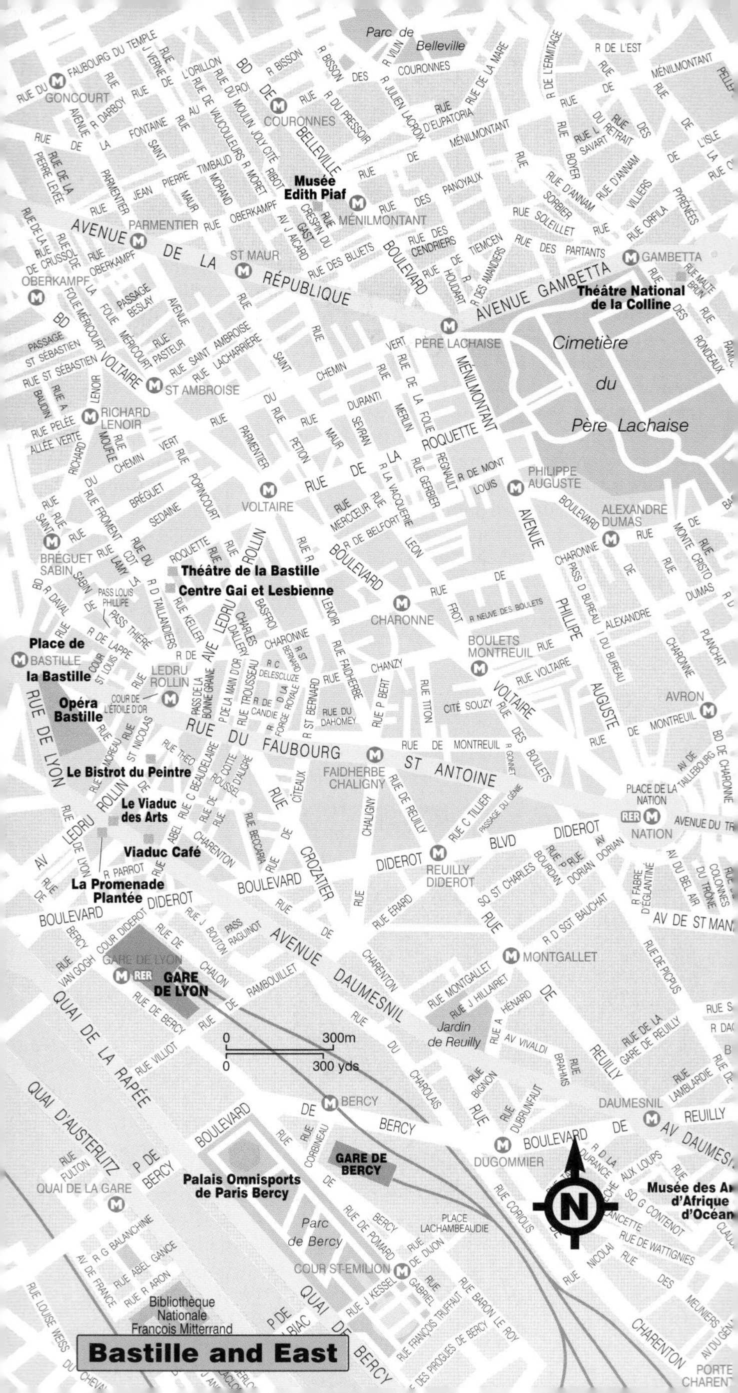
Bastille and East
Parc de Belleville
Musée Edith Piaf
Théâtre National de la Colline
Cimetière du Père Lachaise
Théâtre de la Bastille
Centre Gai et Lesbienne
Place de la Bastille
Opéra Bastille
Le Bistrot du Peintre
Le Viaduc des Arts
Viaduc Café
La Promenade Plantée
GARE DE LYON
Jardin de Reuilly
GARE DE BERCY
Palais Omnisports de Paris Bercy
Parc de Bercy
Bibliothèque Nationale Francois Mitterrand
Musée des Arts d'Afrique et d'Océanie
GONCOURT
COURONNES
MÉNILMONTANT
PARMENTIER
ST MAUR
OBERKAMPF
GAMBETTA
PÈRE LACHAISE
ST AMBROISE
RICHARD LENOIR
PHILIPPE AUGUSTE
VOLTAIRE
ALEXANDRE DUMAS
BRÉGUET SABIN
CHARONNE
BOULETS MONTREUIL
BASTILLE
LEDRU ROLLIN
AVRON
FAIDHERBE CHALIGNY
NATION
REUILLY DIDEROT
MONTGALLET
GARE DE LYON
BERCY
DAUGMESNIL
DUGOMMIER
QUAI DE LA GARE
COUR ST-EMILION
AVENUE DE LA RÉPUBLIQUE
AVENUE GAMBETTA
RUE DU FAUBOURG ST ANTOINE
AVENUE DAUMESNIL
BOULEVARD DIDEROT
QUAI DE LA RAPÉE
QUAI D'AUSTERLITZ
RUE DE LYON
0 300m
0 300 yds

the Viaduc des Arts is located at number 15. This disused railway arch has been transformed into a collection of crafts shops featuring everything from contemporary furniture to smaller *objets d'art*. The Viaduc Café (see Out to Lunch feature) is also a great place to stop for coffee before perusing the gallery, featuring some great contemporary design. Above the Viaduc is Le Promenade Planté, a gorgeous pathway filled with roses and shrubs that adjoins the Jardin de Reuilly at ground level. This garden is a favourite location for both rollerblade fanatics and romantics.

At number 116 avenue Ledru-Rollin is Le Bistrot du Peintre (see Out to Lunch feature), a great pit-stop for lunch and conveniently close to the mini gay villages on rue Keller. This is where you'll find the Gay and Lesbian Centre and a growing number of trendy clothes shops. Take Ledru-Rollin Métro, line 8, towards Créteil-Préfecture, alighting at Porte Dorée, where the Musée des Arts d'Afrique et d'Océanie is located. This mammoth museum, built in 1931, houses a great collection of African art and artefacts from intricately carved totem poles to miniature carvings and tribal masks. Head down to the basement, where a circular rail allows you to look down on to a collection of live crocodiles and gaze into giant fish tanks filled with unusual fish.

Out to Lunch

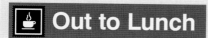

The regeneration of the Bastille area has introduced a good selection of new cafés and restaurants. **Le Viaduc Café** (*see p. 86*), within the Viaduc d'Arts, has a reasonable lunch menu (from noon to 3pm) from around 100F. **Pause Café**, at 41 rue de Charonne (*see p. 86*), serves up modern French cuisine to a jazzy soundtrack for around 80F. **Le Bistrot du Peintre**, at 116 avenue Ledru-Rollin (*see p. 85*), offers Art Nouveau decor and a selection of filling favourites, including macaroni cheese and French onion soup with cheese-dipped bread from 85F.

Taste of the city

OUTLINES

CIMETIÈRE DU PÈRE-LACHAISE

boulevard de Ménilmontant, 75020
01 55 25 82 10
daily 9am–5.30pm.
Père Lachaise

This mammoth cemetery contains thousands of tombs, neatly aligned with peaceful tree-lined lanes. Oscar Wilde is buried here, along with singer Edith Piaf and The Doors' Jim Morrison, whose tomb now needs protection from anti-vandalism police (see Stepping Out, p.15).

Sarah Bernhardt's resting place

CENTRE GAI ET LESBIENNE

3 rue Keller, 75011
01 43 57 21 47
Mon–Sat 2–8pm.
M Ledru-Rollin

The Bastille has become the gay political centre of Paris. This invaluable community resource provides information, advice and a social gathering space to gay locals. Details of social groups across the city are also available should you be planning a longer stay.

Viaduc des Arts

MARCHÉ POPINCOURT

boulevard Richard Lenoir, 75011
Tuesday and Friday mornings
Bastille

Bustling food market popular with locals.

MUSÉE DES ARTS D'AFRIQUE ET D'OCÉANIE

293 avenue Daumesnil, 75012
01 44 74 84 80
Mon, Wed–Sun 10am–5pm
Shop accepts Mastercard, Visa
Porte Dorée

This museum houses a fascinating collection of African tribal artefacts, from towering totem poles to intricate carvings. Head down to the basement to explore the large tanks containing hundreds of varieties of tropical fish and live crocodiles.

MUSÉE EDITH PIAF
5 rue Crespin-du-Gast, 75011
01 43 55 52 72
Mon–Thur 1–6pm by appointment
Admission free; donations welcome
Ménilmontant

Two-room shrine to the 'little sparrow', including her tiny black dress, shoes, letters and photographs. CDs and books are also on sale.

PARC DE BERCY
186 avenue Daumesnil, 75012
Bercy

Neatly manicured lawns, pergolas, roses, a herb garden and an orchard mark Bercy's beautification.

VIADUC DES ARTS
15 avenue Daumesnil, 75012
Ledru-Rollin

Bercy's regeneration into a visitor attraction continues with this series of furniture, ceramics and tapestry craft shops in a disused railway viaduct. The Viaduc Café serves a cool, arty crowd.

Birdsong: The Life of Edith Piaf

Since her death in the early 1960s, French *chanteuse* Edith Piaf has been afforded legendary status for her bitter-sweet songs of love and loss in her Parisian homeland. Many thousands of fans have visited her family grave in the famous Père-Lachaise cemetery, and the nearby Musée Edith Piaf is full of her personal belongings. But Piaf's rise to success was more a case of luck than ambition.

Born on 9 December 1915, she spent her early years scraping a living with her acrobat father on the streets of Paris. It was while singing one day to a crowd of passers-by, that she was spotted by an impresario who signed her up to a future of record contracts and gruelling international touring schedules. In 1936, her mentor, Louis Leplée, was murdered. Suspicion fell on the singer because of her links with Paris's street entertainers, considered to be criminal by many of the upper classes. Despite never being charged with any crime, the singer was shunned by her friends and bookings became scarce.

However, the hiatus didn't last long. By 1939, she was top of the bill again, packing houses throughout the world. During World War II she took an active role in the French Resistance, while German officers cheered her on at the concerts she was asked to perform in. In spring 1940, Piaf starred in the first of several plays, including one written by the legendary Jean Cocteau. On her father's death in 1944, Piaf met Louis Barrier, who became her first ever manager, an association that lasted for the remainder of her career.

Surprisingly, she didn't die a rich woman. The many debts she had accrued during her lifetime were left to her second husband, Theo Sarapo, adding yet another twist to the extraordinary life and career of Paris's 'little sparrow'.

The Opéra – home of music and dance

St-Honoré and Opéra

When we think of Paris, we think of style. St-Honoré and its surroundings, including Madeleine and the well-heeled rue du Faubourg St-Honoré, are home to just about every high-rolling fashion designer in the world. If it's been on the pages of *Vogue*, you'll find it here. Strangely enough, it's also where the French President lives, shops and entertains. The place Vendôme, home to the Ritz Hotel, from where Princess Diana made her final, fateful journey, is one of many fashionable addresses of interest in the area. Central to the square is the Austerlitz column, with its statue of Napoleon dressed as Julius Caesar towering up into the skyline. In case you missed the reference, it serves as a reminder of Napoleon's Battle of Austerlitz in 1805. Beyond the tradition and glamour of the old stands the Galeries Lafayette on boulevard Haussmann, where BCBG (*bon courant, bon goût*) Parisians pick up designer clothes and visitors gaze out over the Paris skyline from its rooftop balcony.

A DAY OUT

New money and old religion epitomize Madeleine's modern-day charm, with its busy financial district and main square dominated by the Eglise de-la-Madeleine (The Church of Mary Magdalene). Built just over a century ago, it dwarfs the traffic around it with its towering, fluted Corinthian columns and Lemaire's ornate recreation of Christ's Last Judgment at its pinnacle. The church is open to the public and well worth exploring.

A gourmand's paradise

Madeleine is also the place to find some of the best food and wine in Paris. Don't miss, at number 26 place de la Madeleine, the world-famous Fauchon (*see p. 69*) for its tantalizing window displays and luxurious food. *Gourmands* will love the selection of beluga caviar and fine French truffles. Its restaurant, overlooking

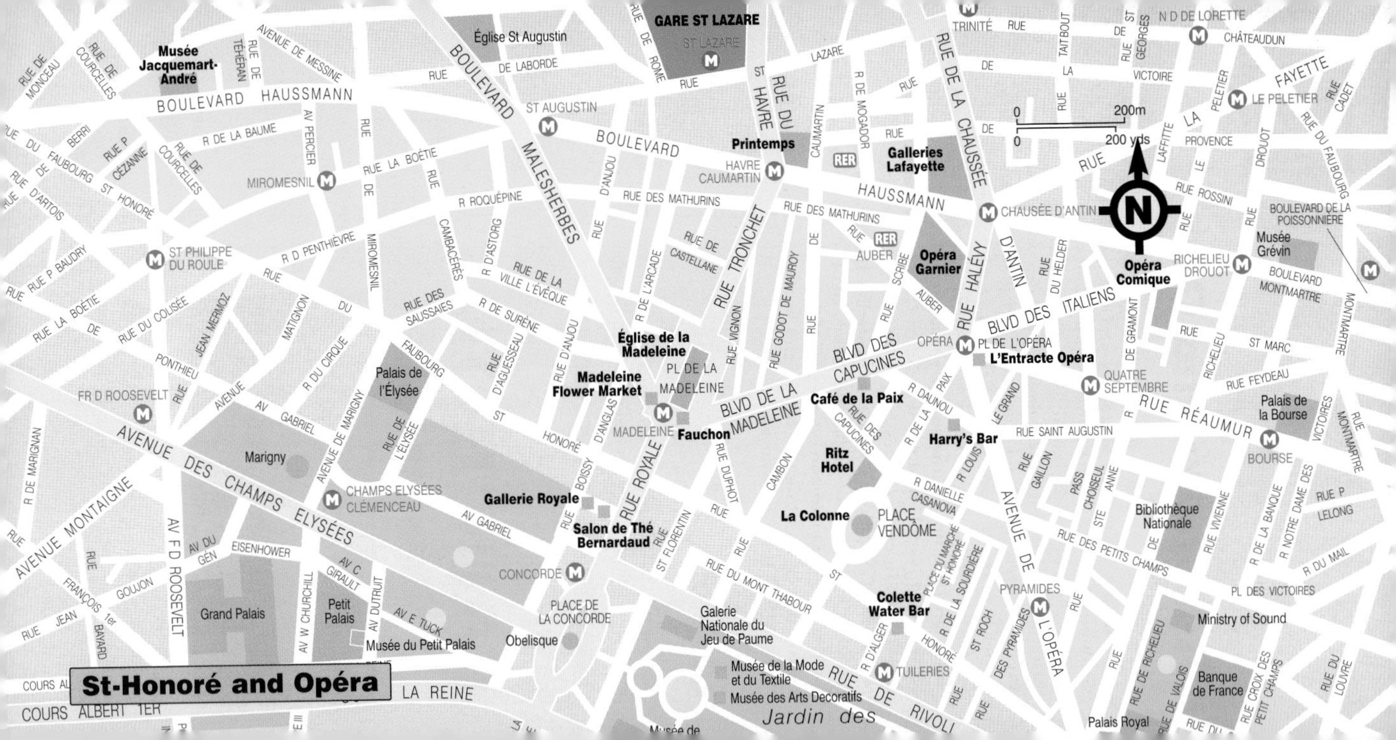
St-Honoré and Opéra
GARE ST LAZARE
Église St Augustin
Musée Jacquemart-André
Printemps
Galleries Lafayette
Opéra Garnier
Opéra Comique
Musée Grévin
L'Entracte Opéra
Café de la Paix
Harry's Bar
Église de la Madeleine
Madeleine Flower Market
Fauchon
Ritz Hotel
La Colonne
PLACE VENDÔME
Palais de la Bourse
Bibliothèque Nationale
Ministry of Sound
Banque de France
Palais Royal
Colette Water Bar
Gallerie Royale
Salon de Thé Bernardaud
Palais de l'Élysée
Marigny
Grand Palais
Petit Palais
Musée du Petit Palais
Obelisque
PLACE DE LA CONCORDE
Galerie Nationale du Jeu de Paume
Musée de la Mode et du Textile
Musée des Arts Decoratifs
Jardin des
BOULEVARD HAUSSMANN
BOULEVARD MALESHERBES
AVENUE DES CHAMPS ELYSÉES
AVENUE MONTAIGNE
AVENUE DE L'OPÉRA
RUE DE RIVOLI
RUE ROYALE
RUE RÉAUMUR
RUE DE LA CHAUSSÉE D'ANTIN
BLVD DES ITALIENS
BLVD DES CAPUCINES
BLVD DE LA MADELEINE
AV F D ROOSEVELT
COURS ALBERT 1ER
COURS LA REINE
0 200m
0 200 yds
N

La Madeleine, is also worth visiting if you're searching for a lavish night out.

Head east along boulevard de Madeleine to the place de l'Opéra, where the Opéra-Garnier stands, surrounded by brasseries and restaurants. The pricey but elegant Café de la Paix (see Out to Lunch feature), a former haunt of Oscar Wilde and Maria Callas, and the more reasonable L'Entracte Opéra provide excellent views of the Opera House. Now used for touring ballet companies, the Opéra-Garnier was home to the legendary Rudolf Nureyev, director of the Paris Ballet from 1983 until his death from AIDS-related illnesses in 1989.

place Vendôme

During his funeral in January 1993, the steps of the Opera House were strewn with white flowers and his coffin carried up into the foyer. From here, take the rue de la Paix south to the place Vendôme, where stands the Austerlitz Column and the now infamous Ritz Hotel. For high fashion, head over to the rue St-Honoré and the rue du Faubourg St-Honoré, which connect just beyond rue Royal. Every designer temple and chic boutique is represented in this intimate corner of the city. Cutting across rue du Faubourg St-Honoré is rue Boissy d'Anglais.

Local bad-boy Thierry Mugler (*see p. 73*) has a shop here, just before the entrance to the Galeries Royale, an elegant collection of boutiques that has its own brasseries. Salon de Thé Bernardaud is a good coffee stop in the heart of St-Honoré. Or drop into the Colette Water Bar, at number 213 rue St-Honoré (*see p. 91*), where you can sip designer waters from around the world. If you're still hot to shop, Galeries Lafayette (*see p. 69*), just north on boulevard Haussmann, is home to chic street styles and off-the-peg designer wear. Its camp and colourful ad campaigns have been a big hit with the boys from the Marais, who flock here for a day picking out the latest looks.

Out to Lunch

As you might expect from an area that boasts some of the world's top fashion designers, the price of food in this part of town is far from cheap. While you will undoubtedly pay a bit more, there are a good variety of more moderately priced tabac doffee shops if you're on a budget. For the gay visitor, **Café de la Paix**, former suppering hole of Oscar Wilde, remains a big draw and the **Colette Water Bar** is the perfect stop-off point for queens into clear skin and stylish packaging.

OUTLINES

ÉGLISE DE-LA-MADELEINE

place de la Madeleine, 75008
01 44 51 69 00
Mon–Sat 7.30am–7pm, Sun 8am–6pm
Madeleine

Commissioned by Napoleon in the early 1800s as a tribute to his Grand Army, construction slowed when the leader fell from power. As a result, the church wasn't completed until 1845. Today, the church is often mistaken as the second home of gossip rag *Paris Match* due to the number of celebrity weddings held here. Inside, Napoleon once again demonstrates his ego with a painting by Ziegler, *The History of Christianity*, with the Emperor pictured in the foreground.

MARCHÉ MADELEINE

place de la Madeleine, 75008
Tue–Sun 8am–7.30pm
Madeleine

Beautiful blooms are laid out along the east side of the church. Getting there early will guarantee the freshest flowers at this market.

MUSÉE JACQUEMART-ANDRÉ

158 boulevard Haussmann, 75008
01 42 89 04 91
daily 10am–8pm
Mastercard, Visa
Miromesnil

Lavish 1870s town house with a fine collection of tapestries and paintings, including Rembrandt's *The Pilgrims of Emmaeus*, as well as works by Botticelli, Mantegna and Bellini. The collection was started by Edouard André and his wife Nélie, who spent a great deal of their time on improving it. The result is rich and elaborate, extending beyond the paintings. The house itself is as much a part of the show as the pictures themselves. The luxurious Le Grand Salon's gold, and the white marble Winter Garden, are just two examples of the museum's finery. There is also a garden and café.

OPÉRA-GARNIER

place de l'Opera, 75009
08 36 69 78 68
daily 10am–4.30pm; tour Tue–Sun 1pm
60F; admission only 30F, 20F 10–25s.
Opéra

Venture where the Phantom of the Opera once walked and wow at the ostentatious interior, awash with gilt, satin and marble, at Charles Garnier's grand Opéra. Built in 1862, the Opéra

Place de la Madeleine

Printemps – a mammoth department store

quickly became the favourite haunt of Paris's elite. Since being restored in 1996, its interior is now used for ballet productions, while the exterior has become a popular visitor attraction in itself. Golden statues and a glorious copper dome complete this slice of perfection.

PRINTEMPS

64 boulevard Haussmann, 75009

01 42 82 50 00

Mon–Wed, Fri–Sat 9.30am–7pm, Thur 9.30am–10pm

DC, Mastercard, Visa, American Express

Havre-Caumartin

Longer established than the Galeries Lafayette, and still just as popular, this mammoth department store has everything for the fashion pack, from designer gear to streetwear. The men's department was recently refurbished. It now boasts the World Bar on the fifth floor, designed by Paul Smith, and an even wider selection of clothes. Don't look for any bargains though. There aren't any.

Opéra-Garnier

Towering over the city

Les Invalides and the Eiffel Tower

Breathtaking views and grand buildings symbolize the area of Les Invalides, stretching out from the left bank of the river Seine. Home to the highest concentration of embassies, ministries and official residences in Paris, this landscape of 19th- and 20th-century buildings sits comfortably alongside one of Paris's most famous monuments – the Eiffel Tower. The Hôtel des Invalides, where Napoleon's tomb is located, was completed in 1767 and used as a home for invalid soldiers. For art lovers, the Rodin Museum allows you to wander around the famous sculptor's former residence, while the narrow streets of the rue Cler market reveal everything edible from cheese to chocolate.

A DAY OUT

The Palais de Chaillot across the Seine

Finding your way around Invalides for the first time can be confusing, largely because it is not the most compact area in Paris. Using the river Seine or Eiffel Tower to guide you can be invaluable, especially as the tower can be seen from quite some distance. Take the Métro to Trocadéro, opposite which you'll find the Palais de Chaillot. The Palais, built in 1937, contains several museums, including the Musée des Monuments Français and the Musée de la Marine. Even if you do not have time to go inside the palace and museums, the Trocadéro Gardens, fountain and grand view of the Eiffel Tower are well worth the trip, especially at night when the fountain and the tower are floodlit.

Cross the Pont d'Iéna to get to the Eiffel Tower, where you can take the lift as far as level three and gaze out across the city. The best time to do this is either first thing in the morning, shortly after it opens at 9.30pm, or much later, after 7pm, when many visitors have returned to

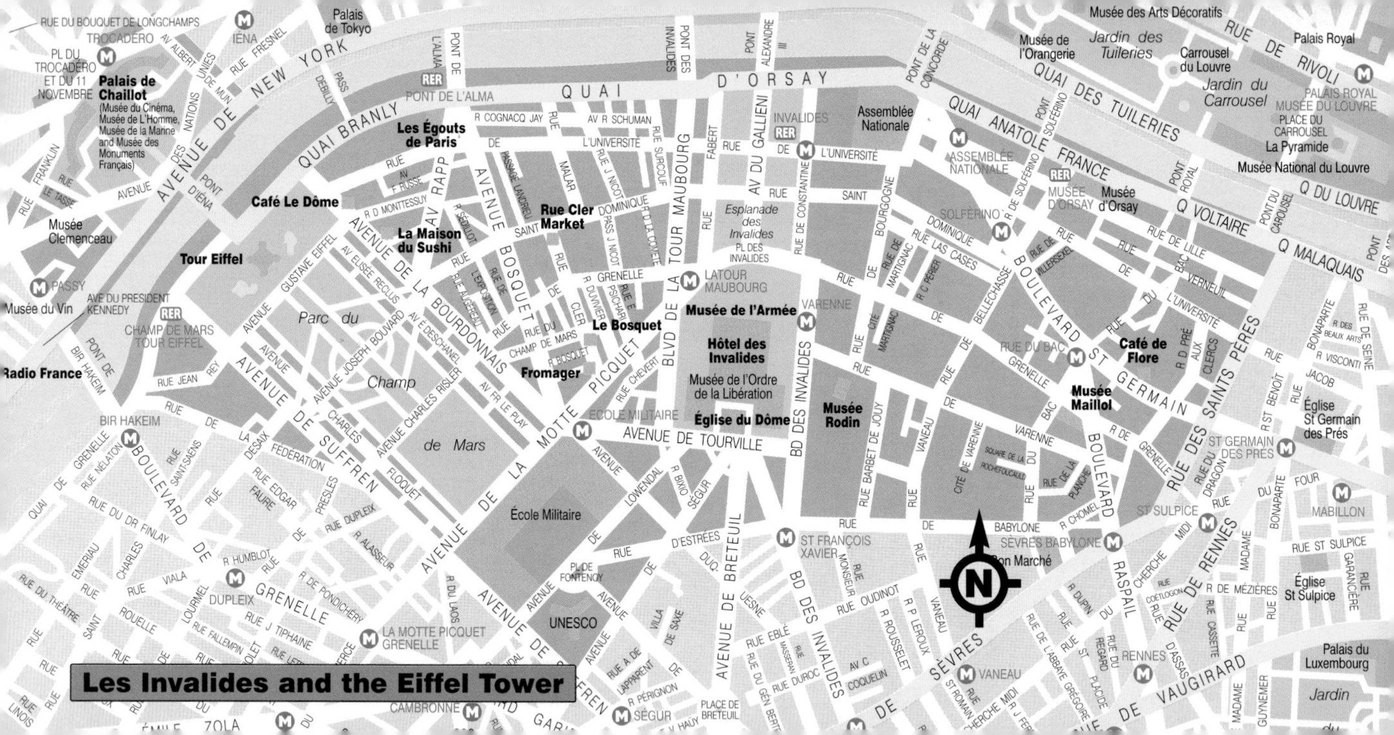
Les Invalides and the Eiffel Tower
Tour Eiffel
Café Le Dôme
Les Égouts de Paris
La Maison du Sushi
Rue Cler Market
Le Bosquet
Fromager
Musée de l'Armée
Hôtel des Invalides
Musée de l'Ordre de la Libération
Église du Dôme
Musée Rodin
Musée Maillol
Café de Flore
Assemblée Nationale
Musée d'Orsay
Musée de l'Orangerie
Jardin des Tuileries
Carrousel du Louvre
Jardin du Carrousel
La Pyramide
Musée National du Louvre
Musée des Arts Décoratifs
Palais Royal
Église St Germain des Prés
Église St Sulpice
Palais du Luxembourg
Jardin
Bon Marché
École Militaire
UNESCO
Parc du Champ de Mars
Esplanade des Invalides
Palais de Chaillot
(Musée du Cinéma, Musée de L'Homme, Musée de la Marine and Musée des Monuments Français)
Palais de Tokyo
Musée Clemenceau
Musée du Vin
Radio France
QUAI D'ORSAY
QUAI BRANLY
AVENUE DE NEW YORK
QUAI ANATOLE FRANCE
QUAI DES TUILERIES
RUE DE RIVOLI
BOULEVARD ST GERMAIN
RUE DES SAINTS PÈRES
BD DES INVALIDES
AVENUE DE TOURVILLE
AVENUE DE LA MOTTE PICQUET
AVENUE DE LA BOURDONNAIS
AVENUE BOSQUET
AVENUE DE SUFFREN
AVENUE DE BRETEUIL
BOULEVARD RASPAIL
RUE DE RENNES
RUE DE VAUGIRARD
RUE DE SÈVRES
BOULEVARD DE GRENELLE
PONT DE L'ALMA
PONT DES INVALIDES
PONT ALEXANDRE III
PONT DE LA CONCORDE
PONT D'IÉNA
PONT DE BIR HAKEIM
N

their hotels. On level one, the restaurant, Altitude 95 (see Out to Lunch feature), has reasonably priced lunch and dinner menus with great views of the square below. A lift takes you right to the top, which can accommodate up to 800 people at once. Here you'll find a meteorological station and aircraft navigation point, but the star of the show has to be the stunning view across the city and beyond.

On leaving the tower take avenue de la Bourdonnais, and cross over via one of the small side streets into avenue Bosquet, stopping off for a coffee or lunch at Le Bosquet at number 46 (see Out to Lunch feature) before heading down into the rue Cler market. Tucked away from the tourist bustle, rue Cler's pretty alleyways, decorated with vibrantly coloured windowboxes and filled with small French restaurants, are a contrast to its busy main street.

A look around Fromager at number 23 is especially recommended for a great selection of cheeses, or take the avenue de la Motte-Picquet towards place des Invalides. Behind the Hôtel des Invalides, from which the area got its name, is Eglise du Dôme, where Napoleon's tomb is located. Circular rails allow you to gaze down upon the famous general's tomb, encased within seven coffins made from a variety of materials, including oak and tin.

On the far side of the boulevard des Invalides is the Musée Rodin, a lavish town house where the artist lived and worked. Now owned by the state, it is filled with the artist's best work. The recently cleaned and restored exhibits are truly awe inspiring. The gardens, however, are just as interesting, with the unfinished *Gates of Hell* and the infamous *The Thinker* benefiting from their place in the Paris sunshine.

Out to Lunch

Whatever your budget, the area between the Eiffel Tower and rue Cler has a good selection of brasseries and restaurants. **Café le Dôme** (*see p. 89*), at number 41 avenue de la Bourdonnais, is situated just a short step from the tower and provides a good stopping-off point for a coffee or lunch. Both locals and tourists are drawn to the café's affordable 50F lunch and 20F coffee specials. Going towards rue Cler, **Le Bosquet** has a restaurant at the front and small coffee shop to the rear, with coffee at around 18F.

For something slightly different, try **La Maison du Sushi** (*see p. 90*) at number 44, offering conveniently packaged sushi and sushimi dishes from 40F. Alternatively, grab a window seat at **Altitude 95** (*see p. 79*), where a fixed-price lunch menu and great view of the city can be yours from 98F.

Lunch al fresco

OUTLINES

LES ÉGOUTS DE PARIS

Quai d'Orsay (opposite number 93), 75007
01 53 68 27 81
Mon, Wed, Sat, Sun 11am–4pm
Closed three weeks in January.
Pont de l'Alma

This trip through the Paris sewer system might not seem the most likely of crowd-pullers but its popularity has taken the city by surprise. A guided tour leads you down into the dank, smelly interior of a working sewer system. A map identifies the streets above as you make your way around. There is also a film outlining the sewer's history, revealing plenty of grisly facts guaranteed to make your stomach churn. It makes the city's 'hole-in-the-ground' toilets seem positively fragrant by comparison.

MUSÉE DE L'ARMÉE

Hôtel des Invalides, 129 rue de Grenelle, 75007
01 44 42 37 72
Mon–Sun 10am–5.45pm
Invalides

Military history from prehistoric times to the present in this lavish town house. Featured heavily are weapons and uniforms from Napoleon's armies, along with many of his personal effects, including his bed and his campaign tent. A collection of maps and documents from later battles, notably World War I, provide a powerful portrait of the war's impact on 'real'

I was just thinking . . .

people. Paintings, including Ingres' representation of Napoleon on his throne, are displayed throughout. Multi-media screens and shocking archive footage complete the history lesson.

MUSÉE MAILLOL

59 rue de Grenelle, 75007
01 42 22 59 58
Mon, Wed–Sun 11am–6pm
rue du Bac

Paintings, prints and drawings by Maillol, collected by his former muse, Dina Vierny, who opened the gallery in 1995. The collection also includes sculptures, tapestries, drawings and engravings, as well as works by Rodin, Cézanne and Matisse, and Maillol's sculptures *Air* and *Harmony*, which feature Vierny in all her glory. The 18th-century hotel housing this treasure house of gems is itself a classic of Parisian architecture.

MUSÉE RODIN

77 rue de Varenne, 75007
01 44 18 61 10
Tue–Sun 9.30am–5.45pm
28F
Varenne

Palais de Chaillot

Rodin's former home, now a museum, is resplendent with some of his best, and best known, work – including *The Kiss*, *The Thinker* and *The Burghers of Calais.* There is also a garden café where you can soak up some of that artistic zeal surrounded by the master's powerful sculptures.

PALAIS DE CHAILLOT AND JARDIN DU TROCADÉRO

place du Trocadéro, 75016
opening hours of Palais and gardens vary
Trocadéro

Built in 1937 for an international competition, the Palais now houses several museums and a recently reopened repertory cinema. The Musée de la Marine focuses on naval and marine history, while the Musée de l'Homme examines anthropology. There is also the Musée du Cinéma, currently closed for renovation. If the Palais is closed, the Jardin du Trocadéro, fountains and view of the Eiffel Tower will be more than enough to keep you satisfied.

TOUR EIFFEL

Champ de Mars, 75007
01 44 11 23 45
9.30am–11pm daily
62F
RER Champ-de-Mars

The symbol of Paris and a magnificent landmark. With a restaurant and great views of the city (see Stepping Out, p. 13).

Place de la Concorde – where the guillotine once fell

www.outaround.com

Champs-Elysées

Running from the place de la Concorde in the east, where the Obélix de Luxor now stands and the guillotine once fell, to the Arc de Triomphe in the west, runs the avenue des Champs-Elysées. On either side, busy fashion chains, brasseries and souvenir stalls encourage you to part with your cash. Nearby, avenue Montaigne displays the more exclusive side of the area, with practically every top designer name in evidence from Dolce to Dior. The Petit Palais and Grand Palais, built in 1900, now house the work of artists from around the globe, while the Arc de Triomphe, built by Napoleon to honour the French army and immortalise his own name, offers some of the best views of crippling traffic in Paris.

A DAY OUT

Given to Paris by the Viceroy of Egypt in 1831 as a way of strengthening relations with King Louis-Philippe, the 3,300-year-old Obélix de Luxor stands in the centre of the place de la Concorde close to Concorde Métro. If the heavy traffic doesn't deter you, cross to the centre and check out the carvings that depict the journey from Luxor to Paris. Walk west on to the Champs-Elysées. On the left is the avenue Winston Churchill, where the Petit Palais and Grand Palais are situated. Each palace houses a range of temporary exhibitions, including paintings, sculptures and furniture. Renovation work might not allow you to go inside, but the exterior of the Grand Palais is particularly stunning, with its glass rooftop and Neoclassical architecture.

On the Champs-Elysées

Follow the tourists along the Champs-Elysées, where you'll find plenty of brasseries and clothes shops. For a reasonably priced cup of coffee and lunch menu, try the Virgin Café (see Out to Lunch, p. 51) or

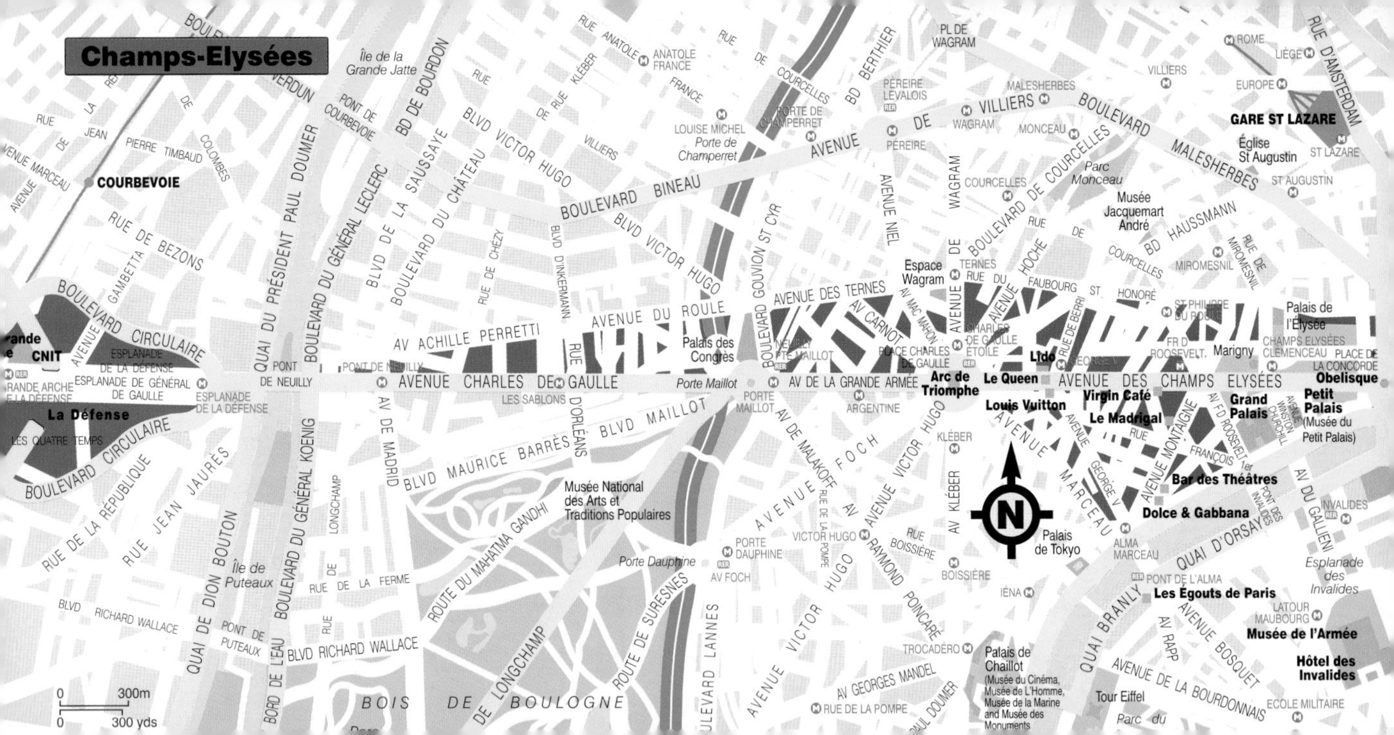
Champs-Elysées
Île de la Grande Jatte
COURBEVOIE
CNIT
La Défense
LES QUATRE TEMPS
ESPLANADE DE LA DÉFENSE
ESPLANADE DE GÉNÉRAL DE GAULLE
BOULEVARD CIRCULAIRE
RUE DE BEZONS
GAMBETTA
PIERRE TIMBAUD
COLOMBES
QUAI DU PRÉSIDENT PAUL DOUMER
BOULEVARD DU GÉNÉRAL LECLERC
BLVD DE LA SAUSSAYE
BOULEVARD DU CHÂTEAU
BD DE BOURDON
PONT DE COURBEVOIE
BLVD VICTOR HUGO
BOULEVARD BINEAU
BLVD D'INKERMANN
RUE DE CHÉZY
AV ACHILLE PERRETTI
AVENUE DU ROULE
PONT DE NEUILLY
AVENUE CHARLES DE GAULLE
LES SABLONS
Porte Maillot
Palais des Congrès
BOULEVARD GOUVION ST CYR
AV DE LA GRANDE ARMÉE
ARGENTINE
AVENUE DES TERNES
AV CARNOT
AV MAC MAHON
PLACE CHARLES DE GAULLE
CHARLES DE GAULLE ETOILE
Arc de Triomphe
Espace Wagram
AVENUE NIEL
AVENUE DE WAGRAM
BOULEVARD DE COURCELLES
LOUISE MICHEL
Porte de Champerret
PORTE DE CHAMPERRET
BD BERTHIER
PÉREIRE LEVALOIS
PÉREIRE
AVENUE DE VILLIERS
WAGRAM
MALESHERBES
MONCEAU
COURCELLES
Parc Monceau
Musée Jacquemart André
BD HAUSSMANN
BOULEVARD MALESHERBES
GARE ST LAZARE
Église St Augustin
ST LAZARE
ST AUGUSTIN
RUE D'AMSTERDAM
ROME
LIÈGE
EUROPE
VILLIERS
PL DE WAGRAM
MIROMESNIL
RUE DE MIROMESNIL
RUE DU FAUBOURG ST HONORÉ
AVENUE HOCHE
ST PHILIPPE DU ROULE
FR D ROOSEVELT
Marigny
Palais de l'Élysée
CHAMPS ELYSÉES CLÉMENCEAU
PLACE DE LA CONCORDE
Obelisque
Lido
Le Queen
AVENUE DES CHAMPS ELYSÉES
Virgin Café
Le Madrigal
Louis Vuitton
Grand Palais
Petit Palais (Musée du Petit Palais)
AVENUE WINSTON CHURCHILL
AV F D ROOSEVELT
AVENUE MONTAIGNE
Bar des Théâtres
Dolce & Gabbana
AVENUE GEORGE V
AVENUE MARCEAU
ALMA MARCEAU
Palais de Tokyo
QUAI D'ORSAY
AV DU GALLIENI
INVALIDES
Esplanade des Invalides
PONT DE L'ALMA
Les Égouts de Paris
LATOUR MAUBOURG
Musée de l'Armée
Hôtel des Invalides
AVENUE BOSQUET
AV RAPP
QUAI BRANLY
AVENUE DE LA BOURDONNAIS
ECOLE MILITAIRE
Tour Eiffel
Parc du
Palais de Chaillot (Musée du Cinéma, Musée de l'Homme, Musée de la Marine and Musée des Monuments)
TROCADÉRO
IÉNA
BOISSIÈRE
RUE BOISSIÈRE
AV KLÉBER
KLÉBER
AVENUE VICTOR HUGO
AVENUE FOCH
AV DE MALAKOFF
RUE DE LA POMPE
VICTOR HUGO
AV RAYMOND POINCARÉ
AV GEORGES MANDEL
AVENUE VICTOR HUGO
PORTE DAUPHINE
Porte Dauphine
AV FOCH
BOULEVARD LANNES
ROUTE DE SURESNES
PORTE MAILLOT
BLVD MAILLOT
BLVD MAURICE BARRÈS
D'ORLÉANS
AV DE MADRID
Musée National des Arts et Traditions Populaires
ROUTE DU MAHATMA GANDHI
ROUTE DE LONGCHAMP
BOIS DE BOULOGNE
RUE DE LA FERME
RUE DE LONGCHAMP
BLVD RICHARD WALLACE
BOULEVARD DU GÉNÉRAL KOENIG
BORD DE L'EAU
Île de Puteaux
PONT DE PUTEAUX
QUAI DE DION BOUTON
RUE JEAN JAURÈS
RUE DE LA RÉPUBLIQUE
0 300m
0 300 yds

load up your credit card at Louis Vuitton at number 101. The infamous Le Queen gay nightclub is found at number 102 (*see p. 95*). Outrageous club-kids and themed party nights are the norm at this pink party spot. More designer names can be found along avenue Montaigne. Even if you haven't the budget, head for Dolce and Gabbana at number 2 (*see p. 73*). Looking like the entrance to a rather chic hotel, this two-storey boutique has pretty much everything from the D. & G. range. At number 6 is the Bar des Théâtres (*see below*), perfect for a light lunch in the heart of this chic city.

Nearby is the area's only theatre, Théâtre Champs-Elysées, where Nureyev once danced and Josephine Baker performed half-naked. The theatre remains well regarded for its classical concerts, drawing a wealthy crowd of enthusiasts and culture-vultures. Although it is closed during the day, an evening performance can be rounded off with a view of the beautifully lit Grand Palais by night.

Head back on to the Champs-Elysées or take the Métro from Alma Marceau to Charles de Gaulle-Etoile, where a tunnel and staircase connecting with the Métro take you to the top of the Arc de Triomphe. Don't try crossing the street above ground to get to the Arc or you'll wind up joining Paris's growing statistic list of traffic fatalities.

Out to Lunch

Whether you're eating, or simply drinking coffee, the Champs-Elysées is expensive. For good value and a view of the bustling street below, head for the **Virgin Café** at number 52 (*see p. 89*), where a chicken, mayo, potato and olive sandwich will cost you around 50F and a coffee around 22F. **Bar des Théâtres** at 6 avenue Montaigne offers a nice alternative, away from the main tourist area. It has a range of main meals, but the brasserie menu is exceptional value (around 60F). Alternatively, you could join the crowds at number 32, where **Le Madrigal** does a roaring trade, despite off-hand service. A *café crème* costs 27F and you can sit outside.

Le Chef

OUTLINES

ARC DE TRIOMPHE

place Charles de Gaulle, 75008

01 43 80 31 31

daily 9.30am–11pm (Apr–Oct); 10am–10.30pm (Nov–Mar)

Charles de Gaulle-Etoile

Striking war memorial commissioned by Napoleon, under which lies the Tomb of the Unknown Soldier. An eternal flame burns here in recognition of the loss of life during World War II (see Stepping Out, p. 14).

GRAND PALAIS

avenue Winston Churchill, 75008

01 44 13 17 17

Champs-Elysées-Clémenceau

Built for the 1900 Exposition Universelle, the Grand Palais is a striking piece of architecture, topped by bronze horse-drawn chariots and a huge glass dome that is illuminated at night.

OBÉLIX DE LUXOR

place de la Concorde, 75008

Concorde

Obélix de Luxor

Given to King Louise-Philippe as a gesture of goodwill by the Viceroy of Egypt in 1829, the 3,300-year-old obelisk stands in the centre of the busy place de la Concorde. Originally in the Temple of Luxor, carvings on the side of the obelisk depict the journey from Luxor to Paris. The place de la

Arc de Triomphe

Concorde was also once where the guillotine fell, taking the lives of more than 3,300 people, including Marie-Antoinette and Louis XVI. The square was later renamed Concorde, meaning 'peace,' to reflect the changing times.

PETIT PALAIS

avenue Winston Churchill, 75008
01 42 65 12 73
Opening hours vary depending on season
Champs-Elysées-Clémenceau

Built along with the Grand Palais, the Petit Palais now houses the Musée du Petit Palais, the city's fine arts museum. Although currently closed for renovation until some time in 2003, the building houses paintings by Impressionist painters as well as Courbet, Delacroix and Ingres, alongside a collection of 18th-century furniture, antiques and medieval and Renaissance *objets d'art*.

Petit Palais

President Mitterrand's impressive marble-clad arch

La Grande Arche and La Défense

Arche de la Défense, Paris la Défense
01 49 07 27 57
Open daily 10am–7pm (last ride 6.30pm)
La Défense

Designed by the then unknown Danish architect Johann Otto von Spreckelsen for the 1989 Bicentennial, the Grande Arche is La Défense's only major monument but makes up for that fact with sleek design, innovative engineering and pure simplicity and size. Standing at 112m, this white-marble clad hollow tube was one of President Mitterrand's *grands projets*.

It contains a lift shaft in which visitors can travel at high speed to the roof, which gives great views of the area. The arch also contains offices and exhibition space, access to which is included in the price of the ticket.

Outside the arch are fountains and sculptures by Miró, Calder and Serra, worth the journey on their own. Towering skyscrapers and the smooth rolling wheels of business dominate the rest of this otherwise uninspiring area. The CNIT building houses major players in the computer business. A new, 40-storey block was recently erected, adding to the area's upwardly mobile, hi-tech image.

View from Montmartre

Montmartre and Pigalle

The Sacré-Coeur-capped Butte Montmartre, the highest point in Paris, and the old red-light district of Pigalle may be close to each other geographically, but little else links its residents except for a mutual loathing of each other. Montmartre, with its winding lanes, small food stores and pretty, villagey feel moves up and away from the bustling neon-lit strip of adult cinemas and table-dancers in Pigalle below. However, Montmartre hasn't escaped the modern world completely. The streets around the Sacré-Coeur are a popular spot for visitors desperate to relive *la vie bohème*. Artists who once sat in cafés idling away their time now make a living painting portraits of souvenir hunters, pursuing them along the street with big smiles and flirtatious words of encouragement. But in spite of its touristification, Montmartre remains a fascinating place to visit, offering a hauntingly beautiful cemetery and a museum that retells the history of the area to help keep visitors' interest alive. While the Pigalle has fewer tourist traps, the Moulin Rouge, symbolized by its towering windmill, still offers up a slice of fantasy to cravers of the cancan.

A DAY OUT

The first thing you'll notice on exiting Blanche Métro station is the world-famous Moulin Rouge, which marks the beginning of Pigalle's main 'sin-strip', stretching as far as place de Clichy in the west and Pigalle Métro in the east.

The artists' quarter

Make your way up the rue Lepic where you can feast your eyes and taste buds on homemade *pâtisseries* at Les Petits Mitrons or inhale the aroma of freshly baked bread at Saint Preux at number 13.

On reaching the junction with rue Véron, turn left and on to rue

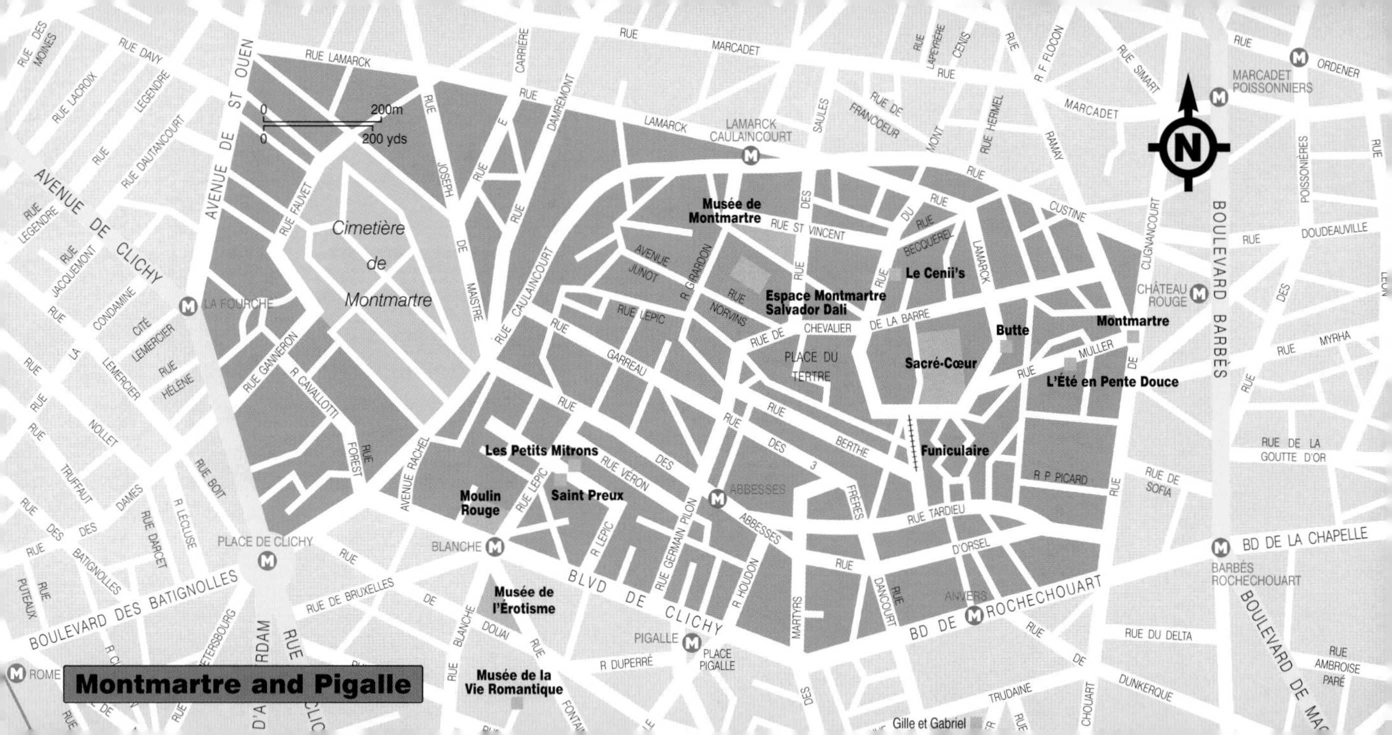

Montmartre and Pigalle
Cimetière de Montmartre
Musée de Montmartre
Espace Montmartre Salvador Dali
Le Cenii's
Sacré-Cœur
Butte
Montmartre
L'Été en Pente Douce
Funiculaire
Les Petits Mitrons
Saint Preux
Moulin Rouge
Musée de l'Érotisme
Musée de la Vie Romantique
Gille et Gabriel
Place du Tertre
0 200m
0 200 yds
N
Boulevard Barbès
BD de la Chapelle
BD de Rochechouart
Boulevard de Magenta
Blvd de Clichy
Boulevard des Batignolles
Avenue de Clichy
Avenue de St Ouen
Avenue Rachel
Avenue Junot
Rue Caulaincourt
Rue Lepic
Rue des Abbesses
Rue Lamarck
Rue Marcadet
Rue Ordener
Rue Custine
Rue Clignancourt
Rue Ramey
Rue des Saules
Rue St Vincent
Rue Norvins
Rue Berthe
Rue Tardieu
Rue Germain Pilon
Rue Véron
Rue Garreau
Rue Joseph de Maistre
Rue Damrémont
Rue Forest
Rue Ganneron
R Cavallotti
Rue Fauvet
Rue Dancourt
Rue des Martyrs
Rue de Douai
Rue Blanche
Rue Fontaine
Rue de Bruxelles
R Duperré
R Houdon
Rue Muller
Rue Myrha
Rue de la Goutte d'Or
Rue de Sofia
Rue du Delta
Rue Dunkerque
Rue Trudaine
Rue Doudeauville
Rue Poissonières
Rue Simart
R F Flocon
Rue Hermel
Rue de Francoeur
Rue Lapeyrère
Rue Davy
Rue Lacroix
Rue Legendre
Rue Dautancourt
Rue Jacquemont
Rue Condamine
Cité Lemercier
Rue Hélène
Rue Nollet
Rue Truffaut
Rue des Dames
Rue Boit
R Lécluse
Rue Darcet
Rue Puteaux
Rue Ambroise Paré
R P Picard
Rue Chevalier de la Barre
Rue Becquerel
M Marcadet Poissonniers
M Château Rouge
M Barbès Rochechouart
M Lamarck Caulaincourt
M Abbesses
M Anvers
M Pigalle
Place Pigalle
M Blanche
M Place de Clichy
M La Fourche
M Rome

Caulaincourt, where some stone steps lead down to Cimetière Montmartre, with its Gothic headstones and family burial chambers. A map at the entrance tells you just who's buried here and where their headstones can be located. About a ten-minute walk to the east is the Musée de Montmartre, at 12 rue Cortot, which recreates the atmosphere of Montmartre's pioneers. It also has a wonderful view over the vineyards and Northern reaches of the city.

Before arriving at the Sacré-Coeur, take a break for lunch. Le Cenii's (see Out to Lunch, below) is a good option. After lunch, follow the throng of other visitors to the nearby domed basilica of Sacré-Coeur. Built to honour those Catholics who lost their lives in the Franco-Prussian War of 1870, the Sacré-Coeur might not be one of Paris's architectural masterpieces, looking as if it has been flung together with mismatched pieces, but the view from the top is phenomenal. Unfortunately, the interior is not as breathtaking. Its original stained-glass windows were replaced with modern ones after being destroyed during the bombing of World War II.

Making your way down from the Butte, take the *funiculaire* train from the Sacré-Coeur to rue Tardieu. Head down the hill and you'll find yourself on boulevard de Clichy in the heart of Pigalle. At number 72 is the Musée de l'Erotisme, a four-storey trip of erotica through the ages, including objects from Africa, Asia and the Roman Empire. Works by famed artist Toulouse-Lautrec, once a resident of Pigalle, are also included, although many of the more contemporary pieces are far more suggestive of the area at it is today. Head west towards the place de Clichy and you'll see why.

Out to Lunch

Finding places to eat and drink isn't difficult when you reach the place du Théâtre just below the Sacré-Coeur, but if you want to keep your spending down it can be difficult. Head for **Le Cenii's** (*see p. 87*), which is ideal for coffee or a light lunch. A dish of *Le Campagnard* (potatoes and bacon grilled on farmhouse bread) is recommended – tasty and satisfying at around 35F. This restaurant also has a range of other traditional French food as well as more ordinary fare, such as burgers and fries. Starters are from 36F, while main meals go from 52F–79F. Alternatively, **L'Été en Pente Douce** at 23 rue Muller (01 42 64 02 67), right at the base of the steps leading up to the Sacré-Coeur, is convenient. It tends to bustle with a mixture of tourists and locals but offers good sized portions for 40F–100F.

Eating out

OUTLINES

CIMETIÈRE DE MONTMARTRE

20 avenue Rachel, 75018
01 43 87 64 24
Mon–Sat 8am–6pm, Sun 9am–6pm in summer. Mon–Sat 8.30am–5.30pm, Sun 9.30am–5.30pm in winter.
Blanche

This beautifully planned cemetery, with neatly kept pathways and staggered construction, remains a big draw for its famous occupants. Degas, Truffaut and Berlioz are all buried here. The entrance to the cemetery has a map, where you can look up the name and plot number of all its residents. Even if you haven't a hero or heroine here to worship, the cemetery is well worth a visit for the beautifully designed gothic headstones and family burial chambers. There are benches available so that you can sit in the sun to write your postcards.

ESPACE MONTMARTRE SALVADOR DALÍ

9–11 rue Poulbot, 750018
01 4264 40 10
daily 10am–6pm
Abbesses

Atmospheric sound effects and the unusual work of Salvador Dalí draw huge numbers of visitors to this basement museum. Along with his better-known work, there are also watercolour illustrations to accompany the books *Alice in Wonderland* and *Dante's Inferno*, as well as small sculptures of melting snails and soft watches. Photographs of the famous moustache can be bought – but they're not cheap.

La Funiculaire

LA FUNICULAIRE

From the Sacré-Coeur to rue Tardieu, 75018
8F; free with Paris Visite pass
Services every 15 minutes.

Useful train service for those people who need to be carried down from the Sacré-Coeur after a long day of sightseeing.

MUSÉE DE L'ÉROTISME

72 boulevard de Clichy, 75018
01 42 58 28 73
daily 10am–2am
Mastercard, Visa
Blanche

Packed with objects telling the story of eroticism through the ages, this seven-storey showcase might not have done much to buck the Pigalle's red-light reputation, but it has a slightly off-beat novelty value. Everything from hardcore postcards and African and Asian *objets d'art* to works by famed local inhabitant Toulouse-Lautrec is included in the admission price. A gift shop sells some unusual presents for the guys back home.

MUSÉE GUSTAVE MOREAU

14 rue de La Rochefoucauld, 75009
01 48 74 38 50
Mon, Wed 11am–5.15pm; Thur–Sun 10am–12.45pm, 2pm–5.15pm.
Mastercard, Visa
Trinité

Paintings and sketches from symbolist painter Moreau cram his former studio. Bizarre maybe but, if you're bored of more traditional fare, this could be just what you're looking for.

MUSÉE MONTMARTRE

12 rue Cortot, 75018
01 46 06 61 11
Tue–Sun 11am–6pm
Shop accepts Mastercard, Visa
Lamarck-Caulaincourt

Small but enjoyable trawl through the artistic history of the area. There is a room devoted to Italian-born Modigliani, who lived nearby, some original Toulouse-Lautrec posters, as well as documents and

Saucy attraction

ceramics. The most fascinating feature, however, is that the studios above were once home to the likes of Renoir, Dufy and Valadon. The views of the nearby vineyards from the upper windows give a captivating view.

MUSÉE DE LA VIE ROMANTIQUE

16 rue Chaptal, 75009
01 48 74 95 38
Tue–Sun 10am–5.40pm
Blanche

Once the home of painter Ary Scheffer, this shuttered provincial villa is not so much a museum of art as of personal belongings. The artist's studio is open to the public, but more interesting are the jewels, lockets and the house itself, which stands at the end of a private alley in a picturesque cobbled courtyard.

SACRÉ-COEUR

35 rue de Chevalier, 75018
01 53 41 89 00
Open daily 9am–6pm
Crypt/Dome 30F
Abbesses

Perched on top of the Butte Montmartre, the highest point in Paris, the basilica of Sacré-Coeur remains one of the city's most popular attractions for visitors if not for residents (see Stepping Out, *p. 16*).

Sacré-Coeur

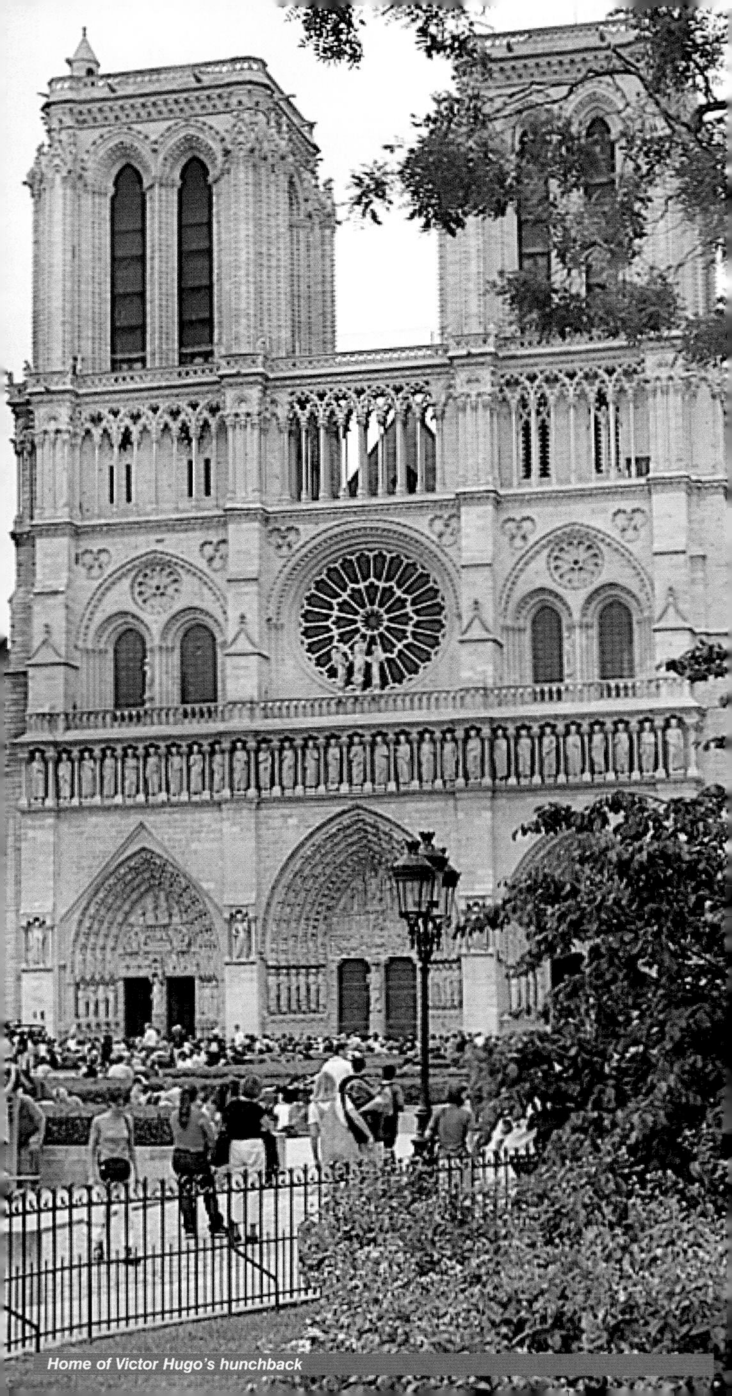

Home of Victor Hugo's hunchback

The Latin Quarter and Iles de Seine

From its medieval streets and cobbled market area on the rue Mouffetard to the many bookstores that surround the famous Sorbonne University, the Latin Quarter is a vibrant mix of historical beauty and modern-day thinking, with students and locals glorying in its old-world charm and bohemian café culture. It was here that the Sorbonne students of 1968 tore up the cobbles in protest and where the Monks of Cluny walked peacefully through corridors of stone in medieval times. Today, the Musée du Moyen Age displays medieval remains and Roman art, while the Panthéon houses the bodies of Paris's famous dead. Across the river, the Iles de Seine are home to two beautiful churches – the famous Cathédrale de Nôtre-Dame de Paris, with its gargoyles, gothic gabled roof and striking views across Paris, and the stunning Sainte-Chapelle, which has twin spires housing the Crown of Thorns.

A DAY OUT

Situated on the Ile de la Cité between Les Halles in the north and the Latin Quarter in the south, Sainte-Chapelle is best seen early in the day before the inevitably extensive queues build up. Take the Métro to Cité and follow the signposts. Inside are a number of religious relics, including the Crown of Thorns, bought from the Venetians by King Louis IX in the 1240s. Head up to the second level for some beautiful stained glass and great gothic architecture. Just east of here is La Cathédrale de Nôtre-Dame de Paris, where Mary Stuart was crowned Queen of France. The church was the inspiration for Victor Hugo's novel *The Hunchback of Nôtre-Dame*.

Browsing along rue Mouffetard

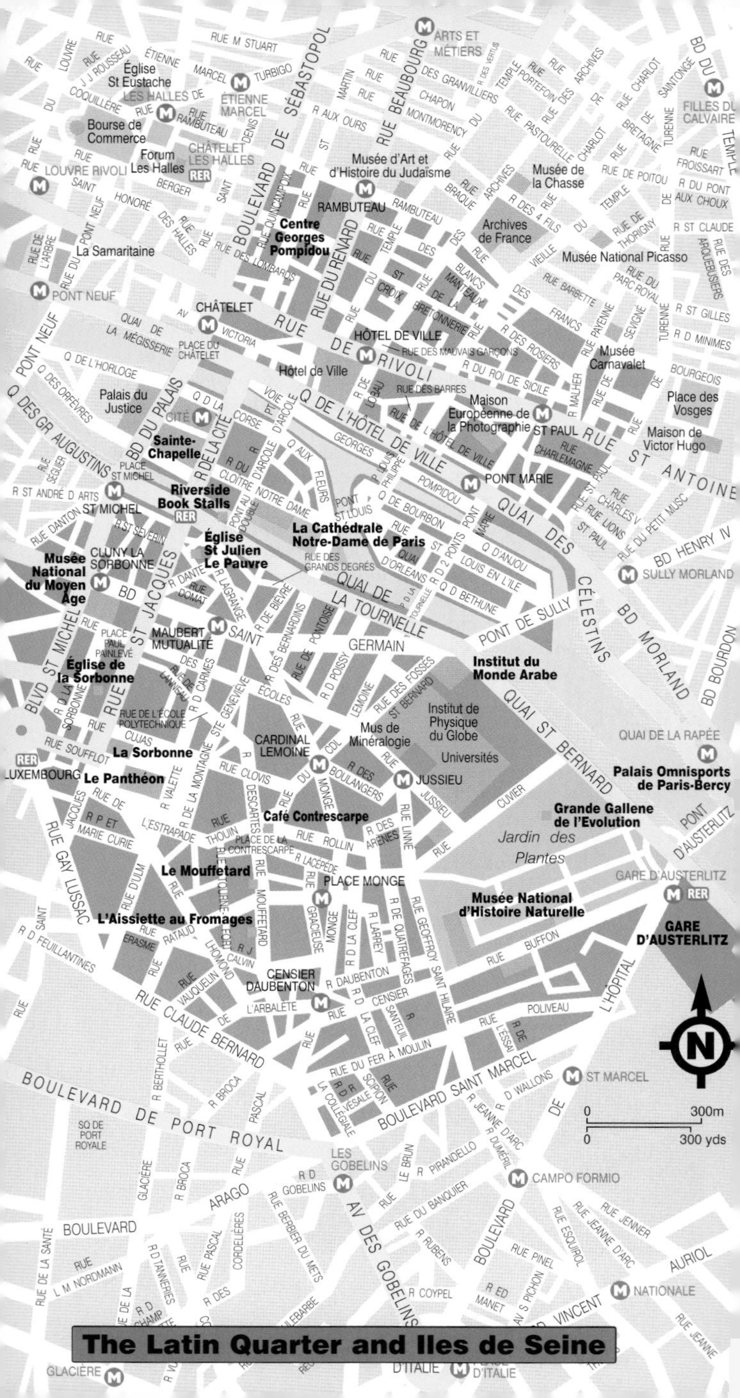

The Latin Quarter and Iles de Seine

The Cathédrale houses some beautiful stained glass and ornate wooden carvings. Head up the 255 steps to the top of the North Tower for some great views of the city and the famous gargoyles. The South Tower contains the 13-ton Emmanuel Bell and an archaeological crypt that explores the evolution of the city, including the remains of medieval streets and Roman buildings. Head across the Pont au Double and along boulevard St-Michel, where the Musée National du Moyen Age is located. The museum is housed on the Hôtel de Cluny and was once the residence of the Abbots of Cluny. The entrance is on place Paul-Painlevé. Inside is a fine collection of medieval art, including the Unicorn tapestries, depicting the five senses through a series of allegories and a room that focuses on everyday life in the Middle Ages.

From here, head for the place de Sorbonne, where you can enjoy coffee or a light lunch at the foot of the University's 17th-century chapel, which acts as a repository for the remains of Cardinal Richelieu. Nearby, the Panthéon houses a crypt containing the bodies ofVictor Hugo, Emile Zola and Marie Curie, among many other notables of French history. You can also see a replica of French physicist Foucault's pendulum swinging slowly from the high-domed ceiling, created to prove that the world rotates.

Next, head east along rue Clovis and rue Descartes into place de la Contrescarpe and rue Mouffetard. A popular place for students, with a plethora of cafés, clothes stores and chatty bars, the rue Mouffetard is most famous for its busy market. The cobbled streets are packed daily with a fine selection of food stalls, including those selling freshly baked *pâtisseries*, fruit, fish and flowers. Visit the market on a Sunday morning for a full taste of the edible delights on offer.

Out to Lunch

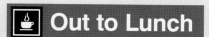

The Latin Quarter's reputation as a great place to eat, drink and socialise isn't misplaced. The small, winding alleys of rue Mouffetard, however, are unbeatable if you want to soak up the particular delights of the market atmosphere. The place de la Contrescarpe, with its circular fountain and view of the market, is a great place to stop for coffee or lunch. The **Café Contrescarpe** serves a good selection of modern dishes and light salads for around 70F; a large coffee costs around 26F. **Le Mouffetard** (*see p. 86*), at number 116 rue Mouffetard, has a selection of heavier dishes at low prices (around 40F) and **L'Assiette aux Fromages**, at number 25 rue Mouffetard (*see p. 86*), serves dishes made from a variety of French cheeses, including a good-value 50F fixed-price menu.

Light lunch

OUTLINES

LES BOUQUINISTES (RIVERSIDE BOOK STALLS)

Along Quai de Montebello, 75005
St-Michel/Nôtre-Dame

This stretch along the banks of the river Seine has an eclectic assortment of books, magazines and prints, including French erotica and ancient-looking postcards.

Bookstalls along the Seine

ÉGLISE ST-JULIEN-LE-PAUVRE

rue St-Julien-le-Pauvre, 75005
01 43 54 52 16
9.30am–7pm daily
Cluny La Sorbonne

Dating back to the 12th century, this church was once a sanctuary for pilgrims, becoming the university church when the colleges left Nôtre-Dame for the Left Bank.

INSTITUT DU MONDE ARABE

1 rue des Fossés-St-Bernard, 75005
01 40 51 38 38
Tue–Sun 10am–6pm
Jussieu

Designed by French architect Jean Nouvel in 1980, this modern, Arabic-influenced glass palace houses a fine collection of Middle-Eastern Art and archaeological discoveries on nine floors. In addition, there is a library and a café selling light snacks and drinks. Don't miss the great views from the rooftop terrace.

JARDIN DES PLANTES

place Valhubert, 75005
01 40 79 30 00
10am–6pm summer; 10am–5pm winter
Free admission; greenhouse 15F
Gare d'Austerlitz

Over 10,000 varieties of plants, greenhouses, a menagerie and a museum are all incorporated into Paris's botanical gardens. Built in 1889, the gardens were closed for some 20 years when the ravages of World War II reduced them to a heap of rubble. Re-opened in 1965, they now include, the Musée National d'Histoire Naturelle and the stunning Grande Galerie de l'Evolution, which has wonderful stuffed animals and rows of brightly coloured birds' eggs. There is also a fantastic 18th-century maze and plenty of new technology to keep the techno-boys happy.

MUSÉE NATIONAL DU MOYEN AGE

6 place Paul-Painlevé, 75005
01 53 73 78 00
Mon, Wed–Sun 9.15am–5.45pm

Shop accepts Visa
Cluny La Sorbonne

Built on top of a roman bathhouse, this 15th-century building is home to a good-sized collection of Medieval art and artifacts, including tapestries, ivory, books and chests. The bath's ruins can be enjoyed, although the cold bath is currently under renovation, set to re-open some time in 2002. The bookshop sells a selection of pricey art books, along with the official guide to the museum and other gift items.

LE PANTHÉON

place du Panthéon, 75005
01 44 32 18 00
Open Apr–Sep daily 9.30am–6.30pm; Oct–Mar daily 10am–6.15pm
Mastercard, Visa
Luxembourg

This imposing church was commissioned by Louis XV to thank Ste Genevieve, the patron saint of Paris, for curing his illness. Completed in 1790, it is now the resting place of many of Paris's illustrious dead, including Emile Zola, Victor Hugo and Marie Curie, who are buried in its crypt. A replica of Foucault's famous pendulum swings silently from the centre of the church, reminding us of the time when he finally proved that the earth rotates about its axis. The original is now housed in the Musée National des Techniques (Science Museum).

Le Panthéon

LA SORBONNE

17 rue de la Sorbonne, 75005
01 40 46 22 11
Cluny La Sorbonne

Famous for its student rebellion of 1968, the Sorbonne has since seen quieter times. After the riots, the authorities split it into several smaller branches, eager to avert future troubles. Many of the buildings that stand today are the result of a re-building programme conceived by Napoleon in the 1800s and carried out by Cardinal Richelieu.

La Sorbonne

The university courtyards remain open to the public throughout the year and are a good place for a wander. The Eglise de la Sorbonne, in place de la Sorbonne, where Cardinal Richelieu's coffin is located, opens for occasional exhibitions and events but it's always wise to phone in advance to avoid disappointment.

Six floors of fashion

All Shopped Out

Parisians have a reputation for being fashion mad, and it's particularly well deserved. The shopping areas along the rue de Rivoli and boulevard Haussmann, where some of the city's largest department stores are situated, are packed with shoppers every day, all looking for the best bargains. Along the more exclusive rue de Faubourg St-Honoré, money appears to be no object, with the very best in designer buys. The top sights below have been chosen to give you a good range of options to choose from, whether you prefer the bargains and bustle of Les Halles, the *haute couture* of St-Honoré or something in between.

Top of the Shops

Boys' Bazaar (Basics, Collections, Videostore)

Everything you need

5, 38 rue Ste-Croix-de-la-Bretonnerie, 75004
01 42 71 94 00
Collections/Basics Mon–Sat 12 noon–12 midnight, Sun 1pm–7.30pm. Videostore Mon–Thur 12 noon–9pm, Fri–Sat 12 noon–12 midnight, Sun 2pm–8pm
Mastercard, Visa, American Express
Hôtel-de-Ville

Everything a gay boy could need, from swimwear and videos to trendy streetwear and accessories. Boys' Bazaar has become the perfect place for shopping, only seconds away from many of the area's clubs and bars. Diesel and Camper are just a couple of the brands on offer, all neatly piled or suspended on rails. The videostore offers all the latest gay porn titles and a good selection of sexy paraphernalia.

Comme des Garçons Parfums

23 place du Marché-St-Honoré
01 47 03 15 03
Mon–Sat 11am–7pm
Mastercard, Visa, American Express
Tuileries

Shielded from the square outside by a shimmering pink-tinted wall of glass, this small but stylish space stocks everything from shower *douche* (gel to you and me) to aftershave balm and the designer's own-brand fragrance, all displayed in showroom style on white podiums. Specially designed as a 'space of exploration,' it manages to remain functional and unpretentious. Prices start at around 200F and escalate fast. But if you're looking for a special gift, there's plenty here to tempt the eye and the senses.

Double Veto

25 rue Vieille du Temple, 75004
01 48 87 52 54
Tue–Sat 12 noon–8pm, Sun–Mon 1pm–8pm
Visa, Mastercard, American Express
Hôtel-de-Ville

Formerly Boys' Zone, this up-to-the-minute clothes store has a good selection of trousers, T-shirts, jackets, jewellery and belts. Unlike Factory's, it avoids club gear, looking to capture the daywear and stylish evening market with a good choice of outfits that can be mixed and matched.

Factory's

3 rue Ste-Croix-de-la-Bretonnerie, 75004
01 48 87 29 10
Mon–Tue noon–8pm, Fri–Sat noon–10pm, Sun 2–10pm
Mastercard, Visa, American Express
Hôtel-de-Ville

Trendy clothes at Factory's

Trendy clothes store for the gay club crowd, which is reflected in the prices and youthful styles. T-shirts emblazoned with logos, jeans and accessories, such as watches and perfume, all pack the ground-floor level of this steel-decked boutique. There is also a basement with a sale rack for those on a slightly smaller budget. Late opening means it is ideal for shopping out of hours. Staff tend to keep a discreet distance.

Fauchon

26 place de la Madeleine, 75008
01 47 42 60 11 | Mon–Sat 9.40am–7pm
DC, Mastercard, Visa, American Express
Madeleine

Fauchon is one of Paris's best known shopping destinations. The windows alone are enough to stir up any appetite but venture inside and you're guaranteed to buy something. Just about every type of food is here, from the best cheeses to the finest chocolate. The Italian deli counter displays ripe, plump olives, Parmesan and Parma ham, and the exotic fruit section is a work of art. You can choose from an extensive wine selection or drink some in the upstairs restaurant, at the same time feasting on the captivating cuisine.

Captivating cuisine

Galeries Lafayette

40 boulevard Haussmann, 75009
www.galerieslafayette.com
01 42 82 34 56, 01 42 82 36 40 (English language)
Mon–Sat 9.30am–6.45pm, Thur 9pm
Visa, Mastercard, American Express

Six floors of top-name designer clothes and just about anything else you can think of. If you're in a hurry, why not go straight up to the sixth floor to the men's department for acres of affordable name-brands. The restaurant offers a range of reasonably priced dishes, and the café overlooks the street below. A few more stairs and you're up on the roof, gazing out over Paris.

Designer label

Jean-Paul Gaultier

30 Cour de L'Etoile d'Or, 75011
DC, Visa, Mastercard, American Express
Bastille

Striking fashions from the gay master of the catwalks in the up-coming Bastille area. Loud and pioneering, many of Gaultier's clothes seem better admired on the peg than worn, but his ready-to-wear lines JPG and Jeans can be accessible and affordable. You can also buy his branded perfume for men for around 300F. Even if you don't buy, the shop itsef is an eye-opener.

Music for all tastes

Les Mots à La Bouche

6 rue Ste-Croix-de-la-Bretonnerie, 75004 | 01 42 78 88 30 | Mon–Sat 11am–11pm, Sun 2pm–8pm | Mastercard, Visa, American Express | Hôtel-de-Ville

Central to the gay district and packed with the best in gay and lesbian titles, this popular bookstore also has a good English language section, along with postcards, magazines and a community noticeboard advertising jobs, items for sale and accommodation. Late opening on weekends means it's an ideal stop-off point after an evening out.

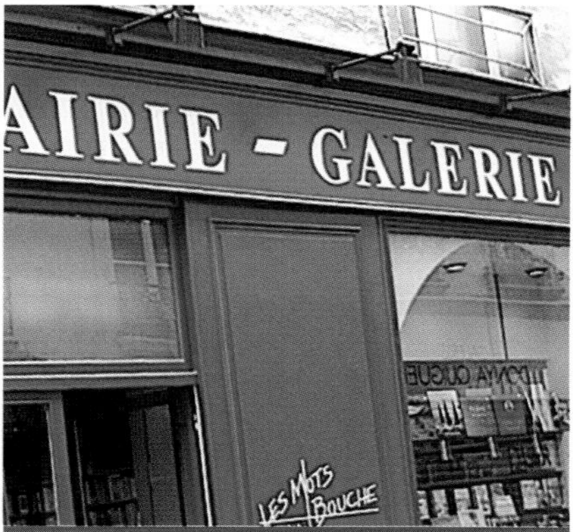

Les Mots à La Bouche

Lucky Records

66 rue de la Verrerie, 75004
01 42 72 74 13
e-mail:lucky.records@wanadoo.fr
Thur–Sat 11.30am–7pm
Mastercard, Visa, American Express

Music store specializing in 'gay pop sounds' from Kylie Minogue and Madonna to Dusty Springfield and Edith Piaf. On first appearance the shop looks small but, when you delve into the racks, you'll find they are crammed with Euro-pop gems. Bananarama's entire back catalogue, Dead or Alive's Japanese releases, even Samantha Fox can be found if you dig. They also stock signed and limited-edition vinyl and have a personally signed Kylie album pinned to the wall. It might not be cool, but it's a poptastic trip down memory lane.

Nickel

48 rue des Francs-Bourgeois, 75004; www.nickel.fr 01 42 77 41 10
Mon 11am–7.30pm, Wed–Thur 11am–9pm, Sat 10am–7.30pm
Mastercard, Visa, American Express Hôtel-de-Ville

Top skin-care specialists for men offer a range of beautifying treatments, including facials at 280F, manicures 80F and waxing 90F–140F. They also stock their own range of products, averaging 160F–200F, as well as other high concept brands such as the Lab Series. The website allows you to order from abroad, so if you're on the go when you run out of goodies, you can restock at the click of a mouse.

Oliviers & Co

28 rue de Buci, 75006
01 44 07 15 43
Mon 2pm–7.30pm, Tue–Sun 10am–7.30pm
Mastercard, Visa, American Express
St-Germain-des-Prés

A shop that is entirely devoted to olive oil and its byproducts, offering neatly packaged items from six countries. The shelves are completely lined with over 15 different types of oil, tested daily to check they remain at their best. You can also buy storage jars and bottles in every shape and size and taste the oil before you buy.

Reciproque

89–103 rue de la Pompe, 75016
01 47 04 30 28
Tue–Sat 10am–6.30pm

Large and well-stocked store with the best in second-hand designer clothes at knock-down prices. Agnes b and Dolce & Gabbana were just two of the names on offer when I stopped in. Most of the stock is in pretty good condition, too. But be warned, if you see something you like, you'd better grab it straight away because you can bet that it won't be there tomorrow.

Sweetman

36 boulevard de Sébastopol, 75004
01 42 77 55 00
Mon–Sat 11am–7.30pm
Mastercard, Visa, American Express
Châtelet-Les-Halles

Outrageous underwear, including slashed vests and briefs in every colour, and skimpy style displayed in all their glory. Gay boys from the nearby Marais and Les Halles area head here with credit cards aplenty to stock up. The perfect gift to put a spark back into your love life. They also offer a mail order service.

Shop Around

GAY NEWS STANDS

NEWS STAND

Corner of blvd de Clichy, 7500
Blanche

Right in the heart of the Pigalle and just across the road from the Moulin Rouge, you can find a good selection of gay magazines, both general interest and adult. A good selection of general titles, too.

KIOSQUE DES AMIS

1 boulevard des Capucines, 75002
10am–10.30pm
Opéra

Gay magazines galore at this popular magazine stand.

KIOSQUE FORUM

10 rue Pierre Lescot, 75001
7am–11pm
Châtelet-Les-Halles

Close to Les Halles gay bar scene, this newsstand is perfect if you want something to read on the métro ride home.

GAY ADULT STORES

IEM

4 rue d l'Arbre-Sec, 75001
01 42 96 05 74
Mon–Sat 1pm–10.30pm
Visa, Mastercard, American Express
Louvre

With three stores across Paris, this is the largest sex shop chain aimed at gay men, offering leather, rubber, magazines, lubricants, sexy underwear and greetings cards.

IEM also has stores at 33 rue de Liège, 75008 (01 45 22 69 01) and 208 rue St-Maur, 75010 (01 42 41 42 41).

Sexy shop

YANKO

10 place de Clichy, 75004
01 45 26 71 19
Mon–Sat 9am–11pm, Sun 2pm–12 midnight
Visa, Mastercard, American Express
Louvre

Adult video store, with booths in which customers can view the merchandise and cruise to their hearts content. Yanko also sells magazines, leather, latex, poppers and more intimate objects. There is another store at 54 rue de l'Arbre-Sec, 75001 (01 42 60 55 28).

DESIGNER CLOTHES

DOLCE & GABBANA

2 avenue de Montaigne, 75008
Mon–Sat 10am–7pm
Mastercard, Visa, American Express, Diners Club
Alma Marceau

Entering this store in the well-heeled avenue Marceau is like entering the lobby of a very exclusive hotel, where style and polite service come as part of the package. Two levels feature the best of D&G's wearable collection and plenty of affordable accessories, including the gay man's favourite *eau de toilette* and a good selection of sunglasses.

MARTIAL VIATIERRO

7 rue Saint-Merri, 5004
01 42 74 00 79
Mon–Sat 11am–1pm, 2pm–8pm
Mastercard, Visa, American Express
Hôtel-de-Ville

Sophisticated street

Thierry Mugler

clothing with an eye for really worthwhile accessories. You could go into this shop and find everything you want, apart from underwear. Manages to be both stylish and street smart.

PATRICK COX

62 rue Tiquetonne, 75002
01 40 26 66 55
Mon–Sat 10am–7pm
Mastercard, Visa, American Express
Etienne-Marcel

The undisputed king of shoes brings his designer goods to the capital of fashion. Choose from a good range of men's and women's styles, including his world-famous penny loafer at around 1,100F.

ROGANEL

23 rue des Archives, 75004
01 40 29 02 20
e-mail ordering: roganel@noos.fr
Mon 12.30pm–7.30pm, Tue–Sat 10am–7.30pm
Mastercard, Visa, American Express
Hôtel-de-Ville

A variety of styles is sold here, from Army combats to trendy club and day wear.

THIERRY MUGLER

10 rue Boissy d'Anglas, 7500
01 43 12 57 57
Mon–Sat 10.30am–7pm
Mastercard, Visa, American Express, Diners
St-Honoré

Top-of-the-range designs at high prices, just off the well-heeled rue St-Honoré. Mugler's shimmering metallic and glass split-level store is pure class, right down to the neatly suited and booted staff and striking window displays.

DEPARTMENT STORES

APRÈS MIDI

51 rue Blanche, 75009
Tue–Sat 10am–6pm
Blanche

A top taste of Italy in Paris. Freshly made pasta, juicy olives and a meat counter with everything from Parma ham to obscure types of sausage and cuts.

BHV

52–64 rue de Rivoli, 75004
01 42 74 90 00
www.bhv.fr
Mon, Tue, Thur, Sat 9.30am–6pm, Wed, Fri 9.30am–8.30pm
Mastercard, Visa, American Express
Hôtel-de-Ville

Less upmarket than Galeries Lafayette but packed with everything from clothes to CDs. Finding your way around can be confusing, and the staff tend to point impatiently when you ask for help. Nevertheless, it's worth a look if you have time.

FAUCHON

26 place de la Madeleine, 75008
01 47 42 60 11
Mon–Sat 9.30am–10pm
Mastercard, Visa, American Express, Diners Club
Madeleine

Opulent and excessive, Fauchon stocks the finest food, champagne and chocolates you'll find in Paris. Beautifully presented and perfectly mannered staff are on hand, encouraging you to dig deep and walk away with a piece of Paris's luxury cuisine.

FLO PRESTIGE

211, avenue Daumesnil, 75012
01 43 44 86 36
8am–11pm
Mastercard, Visa, American Express
Daumesnil

Luxury food at luxury prices. Everything's available, from fresh lobster to caviar and truffles.

PRINTEMPS

64 boulevard Haussmann, 75009
www.smartweb.fr/printemps
01 42 82 50 00
Mon–Sat 9.45am–7pm, Thur until 10pm
Visa, Mastercard, American Express
Havre-Caumartin

Smart clothes for the fashion-pack. Printemps has a long-standing association with Parisian shopping fanatics. Designer clothes are the order of the day, but there is also a good selection of fashionable street-wear. Head for the men's department, where the good-looking Parisian male is as much a part of the decor as the clothes themselves.

SAMARITAINE

rue de Rivoli, 75001
01 40 41 20 20
Mon–Sat 9.30am–7pm, Thur until 10pm
Mastercard, Visa, American Express
Pont-Neuf

Sandwiched between the rue de Rivoli and the Seine, this department store is the only option if you're staying in the gay Marais and can't afford the time to trek up to Galeries Lafayette. The roof terrace bar offers great views.

INTERNET

CLICKSIDE

14 rue Domat, 75005
01 56 81 03 00
Mon–Fri 10am–12 midnight, Sat–Sun 1pm–11pm
Maubert-Mutualité

One of the newer chains to reach Paris, it challenges the smaller internet cafés that are popping up all over the city.

CYBER CAFÉ LATINO

13 rue de l'École-Polytechnique, 75005
01 40 51 86 94
Mon–Sat 11.30am–2pm, Sun 4pm–9pm
Maubert-Mutalité

This is the perfect place to shop if you don't like the factory atmosphere of larger stores. A cool hangout

Outrageous underwear

Newspapers and magazines

attracts a young and suitably trendy crowd.

EASY EVERYTHING

37–39 boulevard de Sébastopol, 5001
01 40 41 09 10
24 hours
Châtelet-les-Halles

An extremely busy place, with queues stretching out on to the boulevard. Easy-everything might not be the most convenient place to log on, but its prices are hard to beat, hence the queues. The only internet café in Paris that's open 24 hours a day, seven days a week.

LE QUETZAL

10 rue de la Verrerie, 75004
01 48 87 99 07

Free internet use during the day.

MUSIC STORES

ÉCOUTE CE DISQUE

12 rue Simon-le-Franc, 75004 01 42 72 13 50
e-mail: encoute.ce.disque@wanadoo.fr
Mon–Sat 11.30am–7pm
Mastercard, Visa, American Express
Hôtel-de-Ville, Rambuteau

Jam-packed with the best in French music. The perfect stop for a musical souvenir.

VIRGIN MEGASTORE

52–60 avenue de Champs-Elysées, 75008
www.virgin.fr
01 12 02 44 21
Mon–Sat 10am–12 midnight, Sun 12 noon–midnight
Mastercard, Visa, American Express
Champs-Elysées

Two levels of music, video and computer games, with a wide selection of both international and French music. Upstairs, the café also serves an interesting selection of dishes from around 60F (see also p. 89).

WINE SHOPS

LE DIT VIN

68 rue Blanche, 75009
01 45 26 27 37
Mon 4pm–10pm, Tue–Sat 10am–10pm
Restaurant open 12 noon–3pm, starters only 5–10pm

The best wines from all over France, with the opportunity to taste the merchandise from 10F–40F. All wine served is with a starter at 20F.

MILLESIMES

8 rue d'Arcole, 75008
01 42 66 98 39
Mon–Sat 10am–8pm
Mastercard, Visa, American Express
Madeleine

If you're at all knowledgeable about wine already, Millesimes will undoubtedly tempt you to the cash register in no time. If you're not, then the staff know just about everything there is to know on the subject, and will cheerfully impart their wisdom.

BOOKSHOPS

GILBERT AND JEUNE

5 place St-Michel, 75005
01 55 34 75 75
www.gilbertjeune.fr
9.30am–7.30pm
Visa, Mastercard, American Express, Eurocard
Saint-Michel/Châtelet

Large chain store with a huge selection of titles on all subjects. This branch also has a good selection of reduced books.

LES MOTS A LA BOUCHE

6 rue Ste-Croix-de-la-Bretonnerie, 75004
01 42 78 88 30
Hôtel-de-Ville

Gay bookstore in the heart of the Marais (see also p. 70).

SHAKESPEARE & COMPANY

37 rue de la Bûcherie, 75005
01 43 26 96 50
12 noon–12 midnight
Maubert-Mutualité

Disorganized it may be, but this famous, old Hemingway haunt still attracts plenty of tourists hoping to unearth some long-hidden gem.

SHOPPING CENTRES

CARROUSEL DU LOUVRE

99 rue de Rivoli, 75001
01 43 16 47 47
www.smartweb.fr/carrousel
Wed–Mon 11.30am–8pm
Musée du Louvre

Busy shopping area near the underground entrance to the Louvre museum. Definitely worth a visit if you're after a good selection of chain stores like the Gap and Virgin Megastore. There are also some smaller boutiques and gift shops and a café overlooking it all.

FORUM DES HALLES

1–7 rue Pierre Lescot, 75001
Châtelet-les-Halles

Larger than the Louvre Carrousel, this one is for the real shopping addicts. Near the Banana and Tropic Cafés (see p. 97), the Forum is swarming with tourists and locals, all looking for the best deal. Get there early to avoid the former and obtain the latter.

Experience the chic surroundings of Parisian bars and restaurants

Eating Out

The Parisians' love of good food is legendary, and Paris is full of places to get your culinary fix. From small, intimate bistros to fashionable eateries, you're never far away from a good meal in the French capital. Gay travellers are particularly well catered for within the Marais and Les Halles areas, where restaurants such as L'Amazonial and the Open Café Bar offer a distinctively gay ambience, right down to the cute waiters and snappy decor.

Cream of the Cuisine

Altitude 95

Eiffel Tower, Level One, Champ-de-Mars, 75007 | 01 45 55 20 04
| daily 12 noon–3pm, 7pm–11pm. | AmEx, MasterCard, Visa
| RER Champ-de-Mars

Despite its busy location, Altitude 95 manages to steer clear of the bustle below, with calm, friendly service and a queue-jump for those wishing to book a table. Altitude 95 is designed to complement the Eiffel Tower's metallic structure, using a riveted beam ceiling and seats by the window to ensure a good view. The duo meal includes one entrée, main course and dessert, excluding drinks, for 98F. Starters are from 59F, mains from 68F. Dishes run the gamut from prairie oysters, baked fish and mashed potatoes to a blanquette of veal with morel mushrooms and carrots. If you're simply after good food, there are plenty of places to temp your taste buds, but if it's atmosphere you're after, head skyward for a meal you won't forget.

The following price guides have been used for eating out and indicate the price for a main course :

(1) = cheap = under 100F

(2) = moderate = 100F – 200F

(3) = expensive = over 200F

Brasserie Bofinger

Bofinger

5 rue de la Bastille, 75004
01 42 72 87 82
Mon–Fri 12 noon–3pm, 6.30pm–1am, Sat, Sun 12 noon–1am DC, Masterc Visa, American Express Bastille

The 'oldest brasserie in Paris' remains steeped in the history that made its name with a stained-glass dome dominating the centre of the room an a traditional menu. Bought by the Flo chain of brasseries in 1996, regulars believed its heyday to be over, but visito and Parisians alike still flock here for the ambience as much as the food. The service may be no-nonsense, but the food is tasty and filling if a little over-priced (the set menu is 189F). But if you want to capture a dash of old-time Paree, Bofinger's definitely found the pulse.

L'Ecléche et Cie

10 rue St-Merri, 75004 01 42 74 62 62 daily 9am–1am Mastercard, Visa, American Express Hôtel-de-Ville

Known for its eclectic mix of modern and more traditional bistro fare, this cheerful eaterie on the edge of the Marais is broken-up into small rooms, creating an informality lost in many larger establishments. A small terrace allows you to eat *al fresco* and friendly service gives you plenty of time betw courses. Try the steak tartar or dip into the popular Caesar salad. Lunch will cost about 85F. The set dinner menu is 100F.

L'Eglantine

9 rue de la Verrerie, 75004 01 48 04 75 58 Mon–Sat 11.30am–2pm, 7.30pm–11pm Mastercard, Visa, American Express Hôtel-de-Ville

This warm, gay-friendly restaurant attracts a mix of lone diners, couples and groups. A mouth-watering menu has a selection of provincial French starters, including snails in garlic butter, a main course and the best chocolate mousse on the planet – all for around 200F with wine.

At your service

L'Amazonial

3 rue Ste-Opportune, 75001
01 42 33 53 13
Mon–Fri 12 noon–3pm, 7pm–1am; Sat, Sun noon–7pm, 9pm–1.30am
DC, Mastercard, Visa, American Express
Châtelet

One of the hottest gay restaurants in town, L'Amazonial serves a decent selection of modern French dishes for around 150F. Lunches are a more reasonable 68F–95F. Rebuilt a few years ago after a fire, it is here where gay Marais meets, chatters and flirts. The waiters reflect the buzzy-pop atmosphere of the place, dressed in tight white T-shirts and entertaining the boys. On the terrace, tacky stone-effect decor hints at a tongue-in-cheek take on eating *al fresco*.

Maxim's

3 rue Royale, 75008
01 42 65 27 94
Mon–Sat 12 noon–2pm, 7pm–10pm
DC, Mastercard, Visa, American Express
Concorde

World famous and dripping with nostalgia, Maxim's manages to retain its air of sophistication (and its pricey menu), despite seeming a little past its prime. New chef Bruno Stril, formerly at the Café de Paris, brings an air of modernity to the menu, attracting new clients but keeping the traditionalists happy. Essentially, Maxim's is a place for people with an eye for something special.

Head for the sixth floor

Georges at Centre Pompidou

Sixth floor, rue Rambuteau, 75004
map p. 62
01 44 78 47 99 Mon, Wed–Sun 12 noon–2am
DC, Mastercard, Visa, American Express Châtelet-Les-Halles

Currently the hippest cool spot in town, Georges, on the sixth floor of the Pompidou Centre, has built itself quite a reputation since opening in February 2000. Looking like a converted loft space with gleaming steel, aluminium pods and translucent tables lit from below, there's plenty here to catch the eye. Cute waiters move swiftly and efficiently between tables, serving-up contemporary dishes to an up-to-the-minute soundtrack. Sit by the window for a great view of Paris or, even better, out on the terrace, where a mixed crowd of smart thirty-somethings and bright young things enjoy anything from omelettes or club sandwiches to Tandoori monkfish or seared tuna. Its proximity to the Marais also makes it the perfect place for gay boys to practise their posing skills before hitting the bars.

Open Café Bar

17 rue des Archives, 75004
01 48 87 54 02
Mon–Sun 12 noon–12 midnight
Mastercard, Visa, American Express Hôtel-de-Ville

One of the few Marais bar/cafés with outside seating, Open is awash with friendly local and foreign faces attracted to the good, if a little simple, food. Sandwiches and salads are moderately priced at around 50F. The seating is arranged so that most people are able to get a good view of the street outside: perfect in the evening when the area livens up. Its prime position at the crossroads with 'gay street', rue Ste-Croix-de-la-Bretonnerie, makes it a wonderful vantage point to watch the world (and the men) go by.

Pain Vin Fromage

3 rue Geoffroy L'Angevin, 75004
01 42 74 07 52
Mon–Sat 7pm–12 midnight
Mastercard, Visa, American Express
Rambuteau

With a wide selection of over 60 different cheeses on the menu, this is the ultimate in French cuisine. Well-informed waiters recommend the right combinations of dishes and wines. The fixed menu is 115F; extremely reasonable for its position behind the touristy Pompidou Centre. Cozy and relaxed, you can dip into four different types of fondue or snack on a salad.

Au Tibourg

Tradition with a twist

29 rue du Bourg-Tibourg, 75004
www.autibourg.com
01 42 74 45 25
daily 12 noon–3pm, 7pm–11.30pm
Mastercard, Visa, American Express
Hôtel-de-Ville

Tucked away from the main gay streets (but opposite a gay sauna), Au Tibourg is a true find. Its traditional appearance may give the impression that the food will follow suit, but the menu's more traditional dishes are tempered with a modern twist, including crab- and salmon-stuffed pasta with a saffron topping (56F) and crayfish and seafood charlotte (149F). They don't sell wine by the half-bottle, but it's worth asking the waiter. They also have a cheaper three-course option for 120F. Wine starts at 50F.

MARAIS

AMADÉO

19 rue François-Miron, 75004
01 48 87 01 02
Mon 8pm–11pm, Tue-Thur 12 noon–2am, 8pm–11pm, Fri–Sat 12 noon–2pm, 8pm–11.30pm
Mastercard, Visa
St-Paul/Hôtel-de-Ville

With classical music (Mozart made his Parisian debut in this area) and a live opera singer twice a month, Amadéo aims at a particular type of Marais crowd. Its reputation as something of a secret bears this out. The menu includes goat's cheese ravioli and *foie gras*.

COFFEE SHOP CENTRAL

3 rue Ste-Croix-de-la-Bretonnerie, 75004
01 42 74 24 21
daily 12 noon–12 midnight
Hôtel-de-Ville

Gay snacks, coffee and alcohol for the men of the Marais. The music is Madonna and Robbie Williams, with reasonable food, including salads, sandwiches, egg, bacon and sausage for around 50F. They also stock all the gay free magazines, which you can peruse at leisure.

EQUINOX

33–35 rue des Rosiers, 75004
01 42 71 92 41
Mastercard, Visa
Hôtel-de-Ville

Tasty French cuisine on the edge of the gay Marais, with wine by the bottle, half-bottle or glass. The food ranges from light Camembert salad to heavier dishes, such as beef in a rich garlic sauce. Avoid the table nearest the door if you want your food to stay hot.

GOLDENBERGS

7 rue des Rosiers, 75004
01 48 87 20 16
daily 8.30pm–12 midnight
DC, Mastercard, Visa, American Express
St-Paul

A famed Jewish restaurant that was the site of a terrorist attack in 1982. A mixture of Sephardic and Ashkenazi dishes cover the Jewish diaspora. You should expect to pay around 150F-200F.

OKAWA

40 rue Vieille du Temple, 75004
01 48 04 30 69
Mon–Sat 7pm–1am
Hôtel-de-Ville

Canadian-style bar with a good, if simple, selection of cuisine (see also bars and clubs, p. 96.)

L'OPEN COFFEE SHOP

15 rue des Archives, 75004
01 48 87 54 02
daily 11am–2am
Hôtel-de-Ville

Sandwiched between Le Cox and Open Bar, this narrow, dimly lit café/restaurant serves a good selection of salads and specials to a young Marais crowd. The waiters are efficient and friendly, but the exuberant kitchen staff can be a bit too much. If you prefer somewhere sedate to eat, better look elsewhere.

LE PETIT PICARD

42 rue Ste-Croix-de-la-Bretonnerie, 75004
01 42 78 54 03
Tue–Sun 12noon–2pm, 7pm–11.30pm
Mastercard, Visa
Hôtel-de-Ville

Hearty dishes inspired by the Picardie region, served-up politely, but cleared away too quickly.
Its position on the busy gay thoroughfare between Les Halles and the Marais means it gets a good ratio of gay diners. Don't arrive any time before 8pm or you'll have the whole place to yourself. The cheaper lunchtime menu is a definite draw.

LE RUDE

23 rue du Temple, 75004
01 42 74 05 15
daily 12 noon–2am
Mastercard, Visa.
Hôtel-de-Ville

Simple gay eaterie serving a mixture of burgers, salads and popular dishes to a mixed gay/straight crowd. Lunch menu can be ordered from 52F.

SUN CAFÉ

35 rue Ste-Croix-de-la-Bretonnerie, 75004
01 40 29 44 40
daily 8am–2am
Hôtel-de-Ville

Café/bar equipped with sunbeds and a nook at the back if you want a quiet lunch. Alternatively, why not sit at the bar, where assorted 20-something locals come for a chat and a quick *café* or *bière*.

LES HALLES

AU RENDEZVOUS DES CAMIONNEURS

72 quai des Orfèvres, 75001
01 43 54 88 74
daily 12 noon–11pm
Mastercard, Visa, American Express
Pont-Neuf

Popular gay eaterie attracting a large percentage of visitors during the day and full of locals by night. Unfortunately, this doesn't mean it's any less busy. Booking is recommended to guarantee more than a glance inside.

LE GUT

64 rue Jean-Jacques Rousseau, 75001
01 42 36 14 90
Mon–Fri 7.30am–7pm, Sat 12 noon–3pm
Châtelet-Les-Halles

Bistro, popular with gay people after something fairly cheap and filling.

DIABLE DES LOMBARDS
64 rue des Lombards, 75001 01 42 33 81 84
www.diable.com
daily 8am–1am
Mastercard, Visa
Châtelet-Les-Halles

Situated in the heart of Les Halles, this busy gay snack bar/brasserie is a popular joint with a young crowd looking for filling international dishes. Fit and friendly waiters are part of the package.

JOE ALLEN
30 rue Pierre-Lescot, 75001 01 42 36 70 13
daily 12 noon–2am
Mastercard, Visa, American Express
Etienne-Marcel

Popular with the theatre crowd in New York and London, Joe Allen's reputation has managed to remain intact, despite what is essentially a small restaurant chain. Situated in the bustle of Les Halles and with English-speaking staff, visitors head here for a perky mixture of French and American food. Plenty of space, a juke box and polite, efficient service mean it's usually busy. Fixed menu 112F–140F.

Sophistication and nostalgia

ZEN
18 rue du Louvre, 75001 01 42 86 95 05
Tue–Sat 12 noon–2.30pm, 7pm–10.30pm, Sun 7pm–10.30pm
Mastercard, Visa, American Express
Louvre-Rivoli

Popular with Japanese locals, this smart taste temple offers up the best in Japanese food, including sushi, tempura and seaweed soup with tofu. Fixed menu 180F; lunch menu from 120F.

BASTILLE AND EAST

LE BISTRO DU PEINTRE
116 avenue Ledru-Rollin, 75011
0147 00 34 39
Mon–Sat 7am–2am; Sun 10am–9pm
DC, Mastercard, Visa
Ledru-Rollin

Regulars crowd into this popular eaterie for a selection of tasty, filling dishes. Its Art Nouveau interior adds to the charm.

LE PASSAGE
18 passage de la Bonne-Graine, 75011
01 47 00 73 30
Mon–Fri 12noon–2.30pm, 7.30pm–11.30pm, closed August
Mastercard, Visa, American Express
Ledru-Rollin/Bastille

Tucked away in a quiet alleyway in the Bastille, Le Passage is a popular eating place for local gay couples who want good food at reasonable prices, though the wine list

Rue Mouffetard

can wipe you out in one sitting. Starters of squid and bean shoot salad or chicken brochette may be accompanied by an inexpensive house wine.

PAUSE CAFÉ

41 rue de Charonne, 75011
01 48 06 80 33
Mon–Sat 7am–2am; Sun 9am–9pm
Mastercard, Visa
Ledru-Rollin

Popular café attracting a lively local crowd.

LE PETIT KELLER

13bis rue Keller, 75011
01 47 00 12 97
Mon–Sat 12 noon–2am
Mastercard, Visa
Ledru-Rollin

Decorated in 1950's vintage style and serving reliable French cuisine, this reasonably priced eaterie in the Bastille can't be beaten for value. A fixed-price menu of 50F–75F buys you a substantial three-course meal, including everything from spinach salad with blue cheese to duck breast in a delectably sweet sauce.

LE VIADUC CAFÉ

13 avenue Daumesnil, 75012
01 44 74 70 70
daily 9am–4.30pm
Mastercard, Visa
Ledru-Rollin

Situated in the Viaduc des Arts craft centre, this is a popular hang-out for many of the neighbourhood's arty types. The good food is tempered by rather slow service. You have been warned.

LATIN QUARTER

L'ASSIETTE AUX FROMAGES

25 rue Mouffetard, 75005
01 43 57 88 34
daily 11.30am–11pm
Place Monge

Specializing in cheese dishes as the name suggests, this basic snack-stop is ideal for the French-food lover on a budget.

LE MOUFFETARD

116 rue Mouffetard, 75005
01 43 31 42 50
7.30pm–10.30pm Tue–Sat; 7.30am–8pm Sun
American Express
Censier-Daubenton

Popular local café in the market area of rue Mouffetard.

LE PETIT PRINCE DE PARIS

12 rue de Lanneau, 75005
01 43 54 77 26
daily 2.30pm–12 midnight
Maubert-Mutualité

Gay romantics spend all evening at Le Petit Prince and it's easy to see why. A warm welcome, and no rush to clear the tables.

MONTMARTRE AND PIGALLE

LE CENII'S

7 rue du Mont-Cenis, 75018
01 42 55 51 52
daily 10am–11pm
Mastercard, Visa
Abbesses

A café just off place du Théâtre, with a good selection of light snacks and main courses. Starters from 36F; mains from 52F.

CHALET MAYA

5 rue des Petits Hotels, 75010
01 47 70 52 78
daily 6.30pm-–12 midnight
Gare du Nord

Hidden behind one of Paris's food markets is this nostalgic homage to off-beat cinematic triumph. Actor Jean Marais ate here and the cocktails are named after the Marais' masterpieces of the silver screen. An all-inclusive menu provides salads and meaty main courses. The lunch menu is around 70F.

CHEZ CATHERINE

65 rue de Provence, 75008
01 40 08 00 36
Mon 12 noon–3pm, 8pm–10.30pm
Mastercard, Visa
Chaussée d'Antin-La Fayette

Relaxed and lost in old-time Paris, Catherine Guerraz's charm-fuelled bistro serves robust classics alongside more modern dishes, personally chosen and replaced regularly. Lace curtains, a tiled floor and a steadily growing clientele of both Parisians and visitors make this a popular place. Booking in advance is advised.

GILLE ET GABRIEL

4 avenue Rodier, 75009
01 45 26 86 26
Mon–Sat 12 noon–2.30pm, 7.30pm–10pm
Anvers

A meaty menu and friendly service await you at this traditional bistro. Gilles cooks and Gabriel waits the tables, while a predominantly gay clientele fill up on beef and other French essentials.

HARD ROCK CAFÉ

14 boulevard Montmartre, 75009
01 53 24 60 00
daily 11.30am–2am
DC, Mastercard, Visa, American Express
Grands Boulevards

Adorned with the clothes and instruments of rock stars past and present, this well known chain of restaurants provides Parisians (and more often the tourists) with a generous plate of American pie. The menu includes nachos, burgers and gloopy shakes, all in large portions. Service is friendly – a plus for when you need help getting up!

NEW PONDICHERRY

189 rue du Faubourg-St-Denis, 75010
01 40 34 30 70
daily 12 noon–10.30pm
Mastercard, Visa
Gare du Nord

Not gay, but if you're looking for Indian food on a budget, then this is it. The set menu is 40F, but if you order from the main menu, you won't have to spend much more than 70F. Try the *dosai* with a choice of meat or vegetable fillings, or fill up on *biryani*.

RESTAURANT FINDER

Burger bar

One of Oscar's haunts

CHAMPS-ELYSÉES

PLANET HOLLYWOOD

78 avenue des Champs-Elysées, 75008
01 53 83 78 27
daily 11.45am–1am
DC, Mastercard, Visa, American Express
Franklin D. Roosevelt

American theme restaurant launched by Arnold Schwarzenegger and Bruce Willis, serving generous portions of American burgers, club sandwiches and Coke, mainly to tourists. The usual memorabilia is here, from films such as *Terminator* and *The Addams Family*, along with enthusiastic waiters and plenty of kids.

VIRGIN CAFÉ

Virgin Megastore, Second Floor, 52 avenue des Champs-Elysées, 75008
01 42 89 46 81
Mon–Sat 10am––12 midnight, Sun 12 noon–12 midnight. Happy hour Mon–Fri 5pm–7pm
Mastercard, Visa, American Express
Champs-Elysées

Impressively laid-out, with solid wooden tables, comfortable seating and a view of the Champs-Elysées below, Virgin's in-store eaterie is reasonably priced for this part of the city. A three-course meal will cost you around 150F, but if you're after a snack, try the chicken, mayonnaise, *pommes de terre* and olive sandwich at 50F. They also sell cocktails for around 50F and are open until late into the evening.

INVALIDES

LE BOSQUET

46 avenue Bosquet, 75007
01 45 51 38 13
www.bosquetwanadoo.fr
daily
Pont de l'Alma

Local brasserie with a restaurant at the front and small coffee shop at the rear. Old-style Paris on a plate. Set menus 75F, coffee 18F.

LE DÔME

149 rue St-Dominique, 75007
01 45 51 45 41
daily 7am–2am
RER Pont de l'Alma

Old-style brasserie with new-style menus in a selection of languages gives you a clue as to just how popular the Dôme's become with tourists. Despite its close proximity to the Eiffel Tower, it remains buzzing with local gossip and character. Try the gratinated onion soup (45F) or the duck *foie gras* with toast (98F), and you'll see why people keep on coming back.

LA MAISON DU SUSHI

44 avenue Bosquet, 75007
01 45 51 24 24
Mon–Fri 11.30am–2.30pm, 6.30pm–11.30pm, Sat, Sun 6.30pm–11.30pm
Pont de l'Alma

One-stop shop for take-away sushi. Ten pieces of *sashimi* for 60F and a lunch menu from 40F. Good value and smartly presented in neat carry-out boxes for style-conscious queens.

SAINT-GERMAIN

CAFÉ DE FLORE

172 boulevard St-Germain, 75006
www.café-de-flore.com
01 45 48 55 26
daily 7am–2am.
DC, Mastercard, Visa, American Express
St-Germain-des-Prés

Once the haunt of the art world's elite (Dalí, Miró and Picasso were regulars), this laid-back, if pricey, landmark now attracts a high percentage of curiosity seekers looking to relive Paris's golden era. Plenty of French cigarettes and Parisian attitude make it more attractive if you're looking for the genuine article. A *café crème* is around 18F – the atmosphere's worth much, much more.

A place to be seen

MADELEINE AND ST-HONORÉ

BUDDHA BAR

8–12 rue Boissy d'Anglas, 75008
01 53 05 90 00
Mon–Fri 12 noon–2am, Sat, Sun 6pm–12 midnight
Mastercard, Visa, American Express
Madeleine

A huge sculpture of Buddha watches over diners in this popular air-kissing restaurant/bar for *poseurs* and players, with prices to match. The fixed menus start at 390F for an evening meal. The lunch menu is cheaper at 190F. Not gay but, if you like your food to be accompanied by a shot of funky spiritualism and style-over-substance, this is the place.

CAFÉ DE LA PAIX

12 boulevard des Capucines, 75008
01 40 07 30 20
daily 10am–1am
DC, Mastercard, Visa, AmEx
Opéra

Charles Garnier designed the interior of this plush and expensive café across from the Opéra Garnier, where Oscar Wilde used to come to eat. Today, it's a popular sight for tourists and gay visitors curious to check out Oscar's Parisian haunt. Lunch will cost upwards of 130F, but if you want to use the toilet it's 2F for the privilege.

COLETTE WATER BAR

213 rue St-Honoré, 75001 | 01 55 35 33 90
Tue–Sat 9am–6pm
St-Honoré

Mineral water will never seem quite the same again after a visit to this bar/restaurant. More than 120 designer bottles are on sale, from the inexpensive to the ridiculous. Perfect for people-watching, as the well-heeled come here for a gossip and a nibble on their light, low-fat lunches.

JOE'S

277 rue St-Honoré, 75008 | 01 49 27 05 54
Tue–Sat 9am–6pm
St-Honoré

A modern menu and a retro feel at Joseph's eaterie, inside his polished store. If you can't afford the clothing, you're unlikely to afford the food.

SALON DE THÉ BERNARDAUD GALERIE ROYALE

11 rue Royale, 75008
01 42 66 22 55
Mon–Sat 8am–7pm
Mastercard, Visa, American Express
Madeleine

Upmarket eaterie inside the sleek Galerie Royale, opposite Thierry Mugler. Prices aren't cheap. A good place for coffee while shopping in the rue du Faubourg St-Honoré.

Café de la Paix

The place to party

out
AROUND

Out on the Town

There are so many gay bars and clubs in Paris that a weekend away just won't cover it. Luckily, many of the best ones are only a short walk from one another in the Marais and Les Halles. If you're looking for a wild night out, Le Queen on the Champs-Elysées is definitely worth the Metro ride. Amnesia Café offers sociable seating areas, while The Mixer Bar boasts DJs on rotation. To help cover as much as possible, I have included a couple of options that open throughout the day. I particularly recommend Open Café Bar for some great food, friendly service and attractive men.

My Top Clubs and Bars

Amnesia Café

42 rue Vieille-du-Temple, 75004
01 42 72 16 94
Mon–Sun 10pm–2am
Free entry
Hôtel-de-Ville

Never forgotten

Relaxed and friendly mix of Parisians and visitors of all ages make this the perfect place to relax, even if you don't speak French. Two levels of comfortable seating and easy-going bar staff cushion the blow for a first-time visitor. Dim lighting adds to the atmosphere and a nook at the rear provides an element of privacy from the busy bar area. During the day, a quieter crowd pops in for brunch or a cup of coffee before meeting friends or making their way home.

Buzzes at night

Le Cox

15 rue des Archives, 75004
01 42 72 08 00
daily 1pm–2am
Free entry
Hôtel-de-Ville

Quiet during the day, yet loud and extremely popular by night, Le Cox is the hot destination for the body-conscious queen of any age. Head there after 11pm, when the pavement outside is heaving with bodies engaged in chit-chat. Inside, the lack of seating and decorative flair is amply repaid with cute bar staff and plenty of hunky customers. It's not a club, but it's as near as you're going to get without dancing.

Look out for the rainbow flag

Le Central Marais

33 rue Vieille-du-Temple, 75004
01 48 87 99 33
Mon–Sun 4pm–2am
Free entry | Hôtel-de-Ville

Attracting a good mix of locals and visitors (many staying in the hotel above), the Central has been going strong for over 20 years and it's easy to see why. Friendly bar staff and a relaxed, neighbourly feel make this one of the prime sights for meeting and greeting.

L'Insolite

33 rue des Petits-Champs, 75001 | 01 40 20 98 59
daily 11pm–5am | 50F Fri–Sat, Wed, Thur, free Sun | Pyramides

A good-humoured disco inferno, with music from the 1970s and a crowd that ranges from the under 18s to the mid-forties. It lacks 'cool', but has a busy dance floor and plenty of social interaction. Finding someone to hook-up with is easy, but finding time to talk between disco stompers is near impossible. The decor isn't impressive (its main feature is a tacky disco ball), but with so much good cheer, who cares!

Folies Pigalle

11 place Pigalle, 75009
01 48 78 25 26
Tue–Sat 12 midnight–7am, Sun 6pm–12 midnight
Fri-Sat 100F, Sun 40F, Mon–Thur free
Pigalle

In the heart of the old red-light district, Folies Pigalle has recently revitalized its reputation, having previously fallen into the tired cabaret bar category. Today things are very different. Get down here on Sundays for the Black Blanc Beur tea dance, where the best middle Eastern, hip hop and salsa, spun by DJs Pipo, Karim and André, are interspersed with live performances and a fun party crowd. Door charges range from around 40F–110F, with the first drink free.

Le Queen

102 avenue des Champs-Elysées, 75008
www.queen.fr
01 53 89 08 90
11pm–4am
80F; 50F weekdays
Champs-Elysées

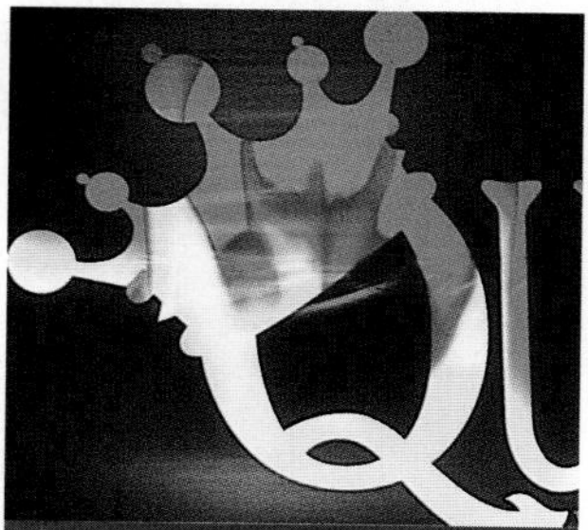
Queen of clubs

Big, brash and packed most nights of the week, Le Queen has become the ultimate in gay Parisian clubbing with a twist. All the top international club nights have guested here, including London's 'Crash'. If confrontation and attitude aren't your thing, there are more suitable and relaxed places to visit. Those who look the part are more likely to get past the doormen. If partying and pouting the night away is your bag, Le Queen's the place to do it.

Mixer Bar

23 rue Ste-Croix-de-la-Bretonnerie, 75004
01 48 87 58 44
Mon–Sun 5pm–2am
Free entry
Hôtel-de-Ville

The only gay bar in the Marais with a heavy focus on club music. Resident DJs on rotation spin the latest underground sounds from a small mixer box above the doorway to an interesting mix of party-hard twenty- and thirty-somethings. A second level allows you to look down at the crowd below, with a walkway that stretches from one side of the room to the other. Free gay magazines and plenty of flyers ensure you'll be busy later on.

Drinking in Okawa

Okawa

40 rue Vieille-du-Temple, 75004
01 48 04 30 69 | Mon–Sun 10pm–2am | Free entry | Hôtel-de-Ville

Right next to Amnesia (*see p. 93*), this fun-packed slice of French-Canadian life is a regular haunt for those looking for surprises. Top French-scene performers and fortune-telling sessions bring in a predominantly male crowd that include a large percentage of American and Canadian tourists. Comfortable seating invites serious lounging. The name means 'peace pipe' in Native Canadian tongue and 'blow job' in French!

Le Quetzal

10 rue de la Verrerie, 75004 | 01 48 87 99 07 www.Quetzalbar.com | Mon–Fri 1pm–5am, Sat–Sun 2pm–5am | Free entry | Hôtel-de-Ville

Situated on the corner of rue de la Vererrie and rue des Mauvais-Garçons (nick-named 'bad boys street'), Le Quetzal is one of the Marais' cruisiest bars. Attracting a predominantly late-thirties crowd, its dim lighting and basic seating provision do nothing to reduce its hot reputation. Head for the creaking spiral staircase, at the top of which are several cosy nooks, if you're in the mood to experience Le Quetzal to the full. If you're here during daylight hours, a second bar downstairs at the back leads into a room with free internet use from 1pm-7pm daily.

A Marais favourite

Open Café/Bar

17, rue des Archives, 75004
01 42 72 26 18
Mon–Sun 11pm–2am
Free entry | Hôtel-de-Ville

Situated in the heart of the Marais, Open has become the cornerstone of the vibrant gay scene in the area. Attracting a young, unpretentious crowd, it's famous for its friendly service and attractive patrons. On the wall a copy of the *Mona Lisa* with the Rainbow Flag over her shoulder adds a touch of humour. Plenty of tables and chairs circle the bar, rarely leaving the customers standing. During the summer months, outside seating adds a *frisson* of excitement, with plenty of eye contact and laughter echoing around the surrounding streets.

All Clubbed Out

LES HALLES

BANANA CAFÉ

13 rue de la Ferronerie, 75001
01 42 33 35 31
4.30pm–dawn
Châtelet-Les-Halles

The trendy Les Halles/Marais set flock to this busy bar to show off the latest fashions and party into the night. The bar staff, however, are not very patient with tourists, so expect plenty of attitude.

L'INSOLITE

See page 94.

LE LONDON

33 rue des Lombards, 75001
01 42 33 44 45
Tue–Sun 8pm–dawn
Châtelet-Les-Halles

Relaxed and unpretentious, Le London pumps out energetic dance music to a fun-loving crowd.

LE TROPIC CAFÉ

66 rue des Lombards, 75001
01 40 13 92 62
4pm–dawn
Châtelet-Les-Halles

A taste of the Bahamas in Les Halles, complete with outside heaters and perma-tan bar men. Similar to the Banana Café. Beers cost around 22F.

LE VAGABON

14 rue Thérèse, 75001
01 42 96 27 23
6pm–dawn
Pyramides

This established and well-respected bar and restaurant is perfect as

After hours at the Banana Café

a post-club relaxer or for a late night out simply chatting with friends (see also restaurants, p. 84).

BASTILLE

ARAMBAR

7 rue de la Foire-Mericourt, 75011
01 48 05 57 79
Mon–Sat 10pm–2am
St-Ambroise

Friendly local bar with chatty bar staff and a laid-back, unpretentious crowd. Happy hours are from 6pm–8pm.

LE GIBUS

18 rue du Faubourg du Temple, 75011
01 47 00 78 88
Fri–Sun 12 midnight–8am
République

Constantly reinventing itself, Gibus is theme-night heaven, without the usual tacky side-shows. The best DJs from the UK play here and it's made its name with visiting club nights like London's 'Queer Nation'. Despite the sound system sounding a bit on the old side, its theme nights remain popular, with top DJs from the UK and France making well-attended visits. Club nights change frequently, so check the gay free press before venturing out.

LE KELLER

14 rue Keller, 75011
01 47 00 05 39
daily 10pm–2am
Bastille

Long-standing leather bar with a strict dress code, a pool table and a welcoming crowd.

MARAIS

ACCES'SOIR CAFÉ

41 rue des Blancs-Manteaux, 75004
01 42 72 12 89
Mon–Sat 5pm–2am
Rambuteau

Friendly local on two floors. Downstairs attention focuses on the bar. Upstairs, comfortable seating attracts a chatty, fun-loving crowd.

Acces'soir Café

ADONIS CAFÉ

5 rue des Escouffes, 75004
01 42 71 15 51
Hôtel-de-Ville

Low-key bar with a mixture of French and English pop and ballads. Perfect for a romantic rendez-vous by candlelight or chatting to friends. There's also a no-smoking section, very unusual in Paris.

LE BAR DU PALMIER

16 rue des Lombards, 75004
01 42 78 53 53
Mon–Sat 5pm–5am
Hôtel-de-Ville

Home to a real palm tree

The most striking feature of this lively local bar is the real palm tree in the centre of it, dominating the room and making a great talking point for the first-time visitor. A pavement terrace, well shielded from onlookers is perfect for sipping cocktails or munching on the delicious all-day menu.

LE COX

See page 94.

LE DEPOT

10 rue aux Ours, 75003

01 44 54 96 96

Mon–Sun 12 noon–8am

Etienne-Marcel

An Aladdin's cave for the S&M set, with a bar downstairs and plenty of darkened passageways upstairs. Everything from hardcore videos to swings, cells and glory holes. Not for the easily shocked.

Call in at Le Depot

Find gay titles at street news-stands

Read all about it...

Finding your way around the scene in Paris is easy, thanks largely to the abundance of gay free magazines available. These can be picked up at gay venues across the city and include listings of clubs, bars, cafés and restaurants, as well as just about every other gay or gay-friendly business. Many of them also have a daily 'agenda', giving you the lowdown on which clubs to visit and when they are at their best.

The most popular publications include *em@le*, *tribumove* and the more political *illico*. *Males A Bars* is good if you want something to slip into your pocket before heading out. Composed purely of a daily agenda, along with a few personal ads and pin-ups, it divides the day into before (pre-club), clubbing and post-club destinations. It also has a section called 'Spectacles' listing current concerts, plays and what's on at the cinema.

If clubbing is high on your agenda, it's also worth checking bars for flyers with reduced entry. *Têtu*, sold at news-stands, provides a broader picture of Paris's gay community (if you can read French, that is), with features, interviews and cultural news.

LE DUPLEX
25 rue Michel-le-Comte, 75003
01 42 72 80 86
Mon–Sat 8pm–2am
Rambuteau

Mixed male/female split level bar attracting a studenty crowd in the main.

LE FEELING
43 rue Ste-Croix-de-la-Bretonnerie, 75004
01 48 04 70 03
Mon–Sat 5pm–2am
Hôtel-de-Ville

Party bar where young people loosen up before hitting the clubs.

LE MIC MAN
24 rue Geoffroy-l'Angevin, 75004
01 42 74 39 80
Mon–Thur 12 noon–2am, Fri–Sat 12 noon–4am
Rambuteau

Busy local bar on the ground floor, dark and cruisy in the basement.

L'OISEAU BARIOLE
16 rue Ste-Croix-de-la-Bretonnerie, 75004
01 42 72 37 12
Mon–Sat 10pm–dawn
Hôtel-de-Ville

Local-style bar in the heart of the gay district with an old Paree feel.

LE PIANO ZINC
49 rue des Blancs-Manteaux, 75004
01 42 74 32 42
Mon–Sun, until 2am
Rambuteau

Long established local attracting a mixture of ages and types. More old Paris than new.

RAINBOW CAFÉ
16 rue de la Verrerie, 75004
01 40 29 05 55
Tue–Sun 5pm–2am
Hôtel-de-Ville

Unpretentious gay bar with performance nights twice a month. Happy hour is from 5pm–6pm and 8pm–10pm.

SUN CAFÉ
35 rue Ste-Croix-de-la-Bretonnerie, 75003
01 40 29 44 40
Tue–Sun 8am–2am
Hôtel-de-Ville

Popular bar/café with a mixed gay/straight crowd. More chatty than cruisy (see also restaurants).

Weekend hotspot

THERMIK
7 rue de la Verrerie, 75004
01 44 78 08 18
Mon–Sun 5pm–2am
Hôtel-de-Ville

Opposite the Quetzal and Rainbow Café, Thermik remains pretty quiet during the week, but hots up at weekends.

A colourful bar

LE TANGO
13 rue au Mairie, 75003
01 42 72 17 78
Fri–Sat 11.30–5am
Arts et Métiers

Unusual dance-athon where clubbers get down to the best in world music, waltzes and the tango.

GRANDS BOULEVARDS

REX CLUB
5 boulevard Poissonnière, 75002
01 42 36 10 96
Wed–Sat 11pm–4am
Grands Boulevards

Converted cinema now hosting one-nighters, with a mixed gay/gay-friendly crowd. Gay nights include 'Speech of Sound' on Saturday (80F with free drink) and 'Massive' on Monday (free). An exceptionally loud sound system and top Parisian DJs attract club kids eager to check out new sounds.

LE SCORP
25 boulevard Poissonnière, 75002
01 40 26 2830
Wed, Thur, Sun 12 midnight–6.30am, Fri, Sat 12 midnight–7.30am
70F Fri, Sat, Wed, Thur, Sun free Mastercard, Visa, American Express
Grands Boulevards

Long established, Le Scorp, formerly The Scorpion, serves up the best in house and dance music. On weekdays a mixed bag of bright young things and ageing club kids head here. At week-ends the atmosphere hots up with drag queens and disco bunnies galore.

MONTMARTRE AND PIGALLE

MEC ZONE
27 rue Turgot, 75009
01 40 82 94 18
daily 6pm–2am
Anvers

Dark, atmospheric cruise bar where practically anything can and does happen. Bare brick walls and adult videos attract an overtly masculine crowd.

Festivals

LES EUROCKEENNES DE BELFORT
03 83 37 99 66
www.eurockeennes.fr
Early July
A scenic lakeside setting plays host to top bands and solo acts from the world of pop.

LA ROUTE DU ROCK
02 99 53 21 79
www.laroutedurock.com
Mid-August.
Established outdoor rock festival with big-name bands from around the world. If you're familiar with outdoor festivals, then you know the score – take a warm jumper, food, hot coffee and waterproofs.

TRANS-MUSICALES DE RENNES
02 99 31 13 10 www.lestrans.com
Early Dec
Four-day-long festival with an eclectic mix of big and small name electronic and pop bands.

A touch of glamour

Playing Around Town

The city caters for all musical tastes, from Grand Opera to pop and rock concerts. World-class venues such as the Opéra-Garnier compete with smaller and more intimate cabaret clubs and legendary names like the Moulin Rouge. Jazz has always found a home in Paris, and the city draws the major rock bands, but classical music remains ever popular.

OUTLINES

AUDITORIUM DU LOUVRE

The Pyramid, Cour Napoléon, 75001
01 40 20 51 86
Mon, Wed–Fri 9am–7.30pm (box office); closed July, August
Mastercard, Visa
Palais-Royal

Classical music concerts and silent films with live orchestral soundtracks.

BOUFFES DU NORD

37 bis boulevard de la Chapelle, 75010
01 42 39 34 50
Mon–Sat 11am–6pm
Mastercard, Visa
La Chapelle

Home to Peter Brooks' experimental work and the world-famous *Carmen*, this unrenovated theatre also hosts visiting companies from around the world and some vocal concert tours.

CAFÉ DE LA DANSE

5 passage Louis-Phillipe, 75011
01 47 00 57 59
Bastille

Former dance hall plays host to touring pop/rock bands from around the world.

Forthcoming attractions

CAFÉ DE LA GARE
42 rue du Temple, 75004
01 42 78 52 51
Hôtel-de-Ville

Theatre on a very small scale, but well-known as the place to be seen when starting out. Gerard Depardieu got his big break here.

CHEZ MADAME ARTHUR
75 bis rue des Martyrs, 75018
01 42 64 48 27
daily, dinner 9.30pm, show at 10.30pm
165F with drink
Pigalle

Famous for its transsexual drag artists, this intimate supper club includes camp amateur dramatics and plenty of audience participation.

CHEZ MICHOU
80 rue des Martyrs, 75018
01 46 06 16 04
Dinner 8.30pm, show at 11pm.
200F with drink
Pigalle

Impressionistic cabaret where small-time performers impersonate big-time stars.

COMÉDIE FRANÇAISE
2 rue de Richelieu, 75001
01 44 58 15 15
daily 11am–6pm
30F, 190F, 65F under 27s one hour before curtain
Palais-Royal

The only national theatre to have its own permanent troupe, the repertoire includes everything from the classical to the contemporary.

ELYSÉE MONTMARTRE
72 boulevard de Rochechouart, 75018
01 44 92 45 42
Anvers

The legendary Paris night spot

Music hall used to be the focus of this age-old venue near Montmartre. Today, upcoming bands play to critical audiences at reduced prices.

GUICHET-MONTPARNASSE
15 rue du Maine, 75014 | 01 43 27 88 61
Montparnasse-Bienvenue

Small fringe venue with the best of old and new acting, writing and directing. Short productions in off-beat styles. Evening performances.

LIONEL HAMPTON JAZZ CLUB
81 boulevard Gouvion-St-Cyr, 750017
01 40 68 30 42
daily 7pm–2am; music 10.30pm
140F with drink
DC, Mastercard, Visa, American Express
Port Maillot

Traditional jazz, soul and gospel at this small hotel/bar.

MOULIN ROUGE
82 boulevard de Clichy, 75018
01 53 09 82 82
daily 9pm–11am
Blanche
Legendary can-can venue with feather-clad dancers and all the glitz and old-time glamour. It continues to do a roaring trade.

Life is a cabaret . . .

MUSÉE NATIONAL DU MOYEN AGE CLUNY
6 place Paul-Painlevé, 75005
01 53 73 78 00
Mon, Wed, Sun 9.15am–5.45pm
20F–100F
La Sorbonne

Medieval music at this museum of medieval artifacts and once home to the Abbots of Cluny.

OLYMPIA
28 boulevard des Capucines, 75009
01 47 42 25 49
Mon–Sat 9am–7pm

The world's major solo artists have all appeared at this venue, including pink fave Edith Piaf and Purple Haze's Jimi Hendrix.

OPÉRA BASTILLE
place de la Bastille, 75012
01 43 43 96 96
Bastille

World-famous, and home to some of the best touring opera companies on the planet, this rather unattractive chunk of art history was created as an opera for the people, but remains popular with the Parisian elite.

OPÉRA COMIQUE
place Boïeldieu, 75002
01 42 44 45 40
Box Office in rue Favart Mon–Sat 11am–7pm
DC, Mastercard, Visa, American Express
Richelieu-Drouot

Operetta and concerts

Charles Garnier's Opera House

at this century-old venue known as the first stop for new opera productions. Admission prices vary. Phone for details.

OPÉRA-GARNIER
1 place de l'Opéra, 75009
01 47 42 57 50
Opéra

One of Paris's major operatic monuments, it's now home to classical ballet. Nureyev used to dance here before storming from the stage during one of his legendary tantrums.

PALAIS OMNISPORTS DE PARIS-BERCY
8 boulevard de Bercy, 75012
01 44 68 44 68
Bercy

This landmark venue, with 16,000 seats and a grass-covered exterior, is located not far from Bercy's burgeoning wine district. It hosts major concert tours from around the world.

PÉNICHE OPÉRA
42 quai de la Loire, 75019
01 53 35 07 77
Mon–Fri 10am–7pm
Mastercard, Visa
Jaur

Boat-bound opera company with links to the Opéra Comique.

RADIO FRANCE
116 avenue du President-Kennedy, 75016
01 42 30 22 22; concert info: 01 42 30 15 16
Mon–Sat 11am–6pm
Free–120F
Passy

Live broadcasts from the French Radio Orchestra, along with an impressive mix of operas and world music.

LE SLOW CLUB
130 rue de Rivoli, 75001
01 42 33 84 30
Tue, Thur 10pm– 3am; Fri, Sat10pm– 3am; music 10pm
Mastercard, Visa
Châtelet

Great acoustics at this cellar bar, with boogie-woogie orchestra and swing bands.

LE SUNSET/LE SUNSIDE
60 rue des Lombards, 75001
01 40 26 46 60
Mon–Sat 9.30pm–4am; music 10pm (Sunset), 9pm (Sunside)
Mastercard, Visa
Châtelet

Home to some of the best jazz and world-music bands in Paris and a few international names. Le Sunside plays hard bop and

Chez Michou

bebop to a knowing musical crowd.

THÉÂTRE CHAMPS-ELYSÉES

See page 51.

THÉÂTRE DE LA BASTILLE

76 rue de la Roquette, 75011
01 43 57 42 14
Mon–Fri 10am– 6pm, Sat–Sun 2–6pm
120F; 80F under 26s. Mastercard, Visa, American Express

Contemporary music and dance with an experimental edge.

THÉÂTRE MONTPARNASSE

32 rue de la Gaîté, 75014 01 43 22 77 74
Edgar-Quinet

Theatregoers' paradise with bar and restaurant.

THÉÂTRE MUSICAL DE PARIS

1 place du Châtelet, 75001
01 40 28 28 40
daily 11am–7pm
Châtelet

Newly renovated, the Châtelet features the best in opera, classical concerts and ballet.

THÉÂTRE NATIONAL DE LA COLLINE

15 rue Malte-Brun, 75020
01 44 62 52 52
Mon–Fri 11am–6pm; Sat 1pm– 7pm; Sun 2–5pm. Box office Mon–Sat only.
160F; 80F under 30s. Mastercard, Visa
Jourdain

Top contemporary drama from around the world, including the best in French writing and direction. The upstairs Le Petit Théâtre includes work by lesser-known writers.

Ooh la la . . .

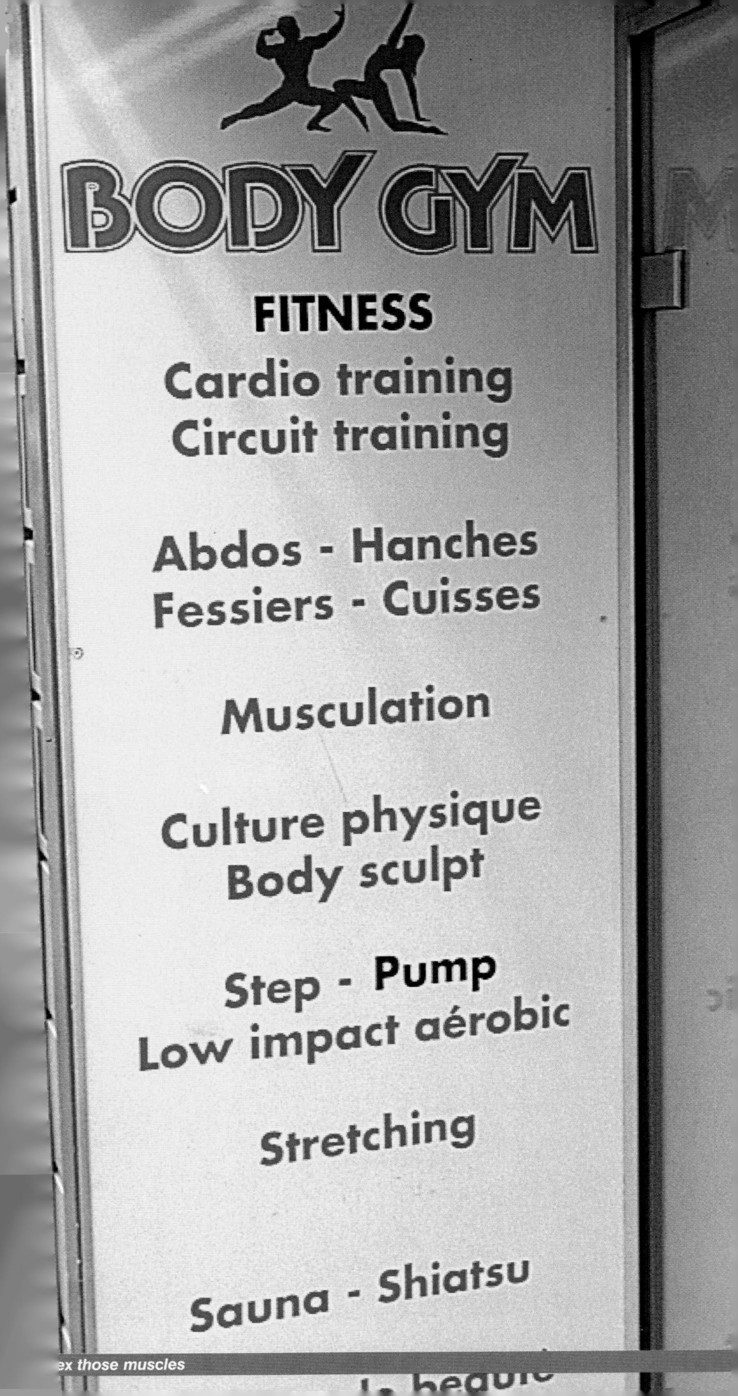
BODY GYM
FITNESS
Cardio training
Circuit training
Abdos - Hanches
Fessiers - Cuisses
Musculation
Culture physique
Body sculpt
Step - Pump
Low impact aérobic
Stretching
Sauna - Shiatsu

ex those muscles

Working Out

Paris has a thriving gym scene, built largely on the premise that exercise and adult entertainment go hand-in-hand. Most gyms here also have Turkish baths, and many have saunas and jacuzzis, too. Some even have their own cinemas, where the latest porn movies from the US are shown. A fair number are situated around the Marais area and all have a high standard of cleanliness. The following choices come with a recommendation from local people.

OUTLINES

ATHLETIC WORLD

20 rue du Bourg Tibourg, 75004
01 42 77 19 78
www.athleticworldmaraisnoos.fr
Tue, Wed, Thur 12 noon–2am, Fri, Sat, Sun 4pm–2am
Hôtel-de-Ville

One of the newer gay saunas to pop up in the Marais, and it's already getting quite a name for itself as a good place to party after-hours for a young, 'athletic' crowd who are looking for more than just a dip in the jacuzzi. There's an added attraction on the ground floor, where a shop sells trendy clothes and accessories.

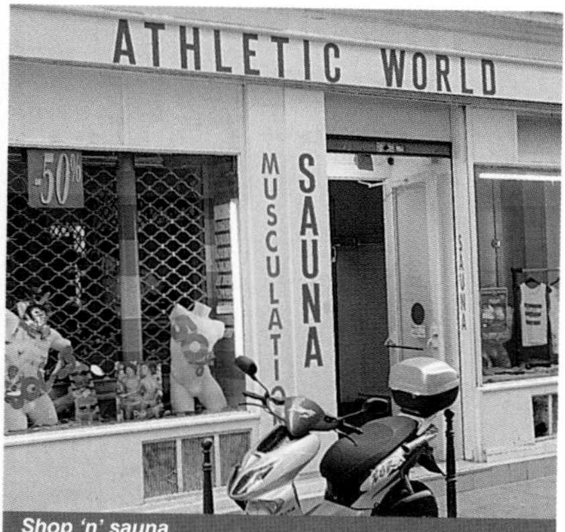

Shop 'n' sauna

EURO MEN'S CLUB

8–10 rue St-Marc, 75002
01 42 33 92 63
Mon–Sat 12 noon–11pm, Sun 1pm–11pm
Bourse

Welcoming, well-established and deservedly popular club with a whole mixture of ages and types, from the under 20s to the over 50s. There are three floors to explore, including a swimming pool, sauna, Turkish bath, sunbeds, cabins and a bar. It's clean and probably one of the friendliest sauna centres in Paris.

IDM

4 rue du Faubourg-Montmartre, 75009
01 45 23 10 03
Mon–Thur 12 noon–1am; Fri–Sun 12 noon–2am
Bourse

Clean, comfortable and spacious, this four-floor gym and bath-house attracts a mix of ages from the under 20s to the mid-40s. Jacuzzi, hot tub and sunbeds with private cabins.

KEY WEST

141 rue Lafayette, 75010
01 45 26 31 74
Mon–Fri 12 noon–1am; Sat–Sun 12 noon–2am
Gare du Nord

Despite being well away from the Marais, Key West remains *the* place to be seen if you're young, fit and on the prowl. Turkish bath, pool, sauna as well as pool tables. Screenings of the latest adult movies from the US are also available. The weekends are exceptionally busy, so if you want to test the water, weekdays are your best bet.

MOLITOR

2 avenue de la Porte-Molitor 50F–70F

Not gay, but this 1930s pool on the edge of the Bois de Boulogne is worth visiting if you like some open-air exercise.

PISCINE SUSANNE BERLIOUX/LES HALLES

10 place de la Rotonde, Niveau 3, Porte du Jour, Forum des Halles, 75001

Far from Florida

Get steamed up

10am–10pm
Châtelet-Les-Halles

Popular local pool, featuring a vaulted concrete ceiling and glass wall with a view of a tropical garden. Not gay, but popular with a gay and straight crowd.

PONTOISE
19 rue de Pontoise, 75005
9am–10pm
Maubert-Mutualité

Popular for its late-night swimming sessions from 9pm–midnight, Mon–Thur, and its reasonable rates. Nude swimming also takes place here on occasion, but this is not a gay pool.

UNIVERS GYM
22 rue des Bons Enfants, 75001
01 42 61 24 83
www.univers.net
Mon–Thur 12 noon–1am, Sat–Sun 12 noon–2am
Palais-Royal

Despite its name, Univers is more than a gym, so don't go in expecting your local YMCA. Apart from a sauna, steam-room and jacuzzi, there's also an in-house cinema. Special parties at weekends for the young and beautiful.

Men only

The Mouse's House

Out of Town

Venture beyond the city limits and you'll discover that a visit to Paris has more on offer than your average city break. A short train journey can land you in some of the most beautiful countryside in France. And while many of the out-of-town attractions, such as Monet's garden and Euro Disney, do get extremely busy in season, they are worth the effort. Alternatively, why not wander around Van Gogh's studio or explore the Palace of Versailles for some wonderful photo opportunities?

Château de Chantilly/ Musée Condé

03 44 62 62 62 | Opening times vary according to season; telephone for details 42F; Montgolfier balloon (03 44 57 29 14) Mar–Nov daily 10.30am–7pm
| SNCF Chantilly, then ten-minute taxi ride Journey time: around one hour

Largely destroyed during the Revolution, the main wing of this French Renaissance château was reconstructed during the 19th century. Once owned by the powerful Condé family, most of the château has become a museum. Paintings by Raphael, Filippino Lippi and a fine collection of portraits of 16th- and 17th-century French monarchs are the main attractions. Outside, Le Nôtre's layout of neat pathways and pools adds to the château's grand appearance. During the summer months, you can also ride Montgolfier's balloon, which provides stunning views of the château and surrounding woodland.

Château de Fontainebleau

01 60 71 50 70 | times vary according to season, telephone for details
| RER Fountainebleau–Avon, then bus marked Château Journey time: around 50 minutes

This luxurious palace was once a run-down Royal lodge until it was transformed in 1528 by François I, who commissioned architect Gilles le

Breton to create an Italianate-style palace in its place. The result is lavish fireplaces, intricate gold panelling and a grand ballroom. Later monarchs added to the palace, creating an eclectic mix of styles, including Napoleon's Empire style and a double horseshoe staircase added by Louis XIII. The countryside in which the palace is situated was once a popular hunting ground. Today it attracts wildlife fanatics and other people interested in the outdoor life.

Disneyland Paris

Marne-la-Vallée | 01 60 30 60 30 | Apr–June daily 9am–8pm; July–Aug daily 9am–10pm; Sep–Mar Mon-Fri 10am–6pm, Sat & Sun 9am–8pm

All lit up

No trip to Paris is complete without an excursion to Disneyland Paris. This 1,943-hectare site opened in 1992 as a replica of Disney's three other theme parks. Since French management took over the running of the park, however, it has become more identifiably French. Strict no-smoking rules have been relaxed to allow staff to smoke within its boundaries when off duty, and a more relaxed European feel has taken hold. With over 12 million visitors a year and plans to open a second park, Disney Studios, in 2002, Disney's European success is assured.

Despite being located some 20 miles from Paris, getting here is easy. Take RER line A to Marne-la-Vallée. The entrance to the park is practically next door to the station. Arriving before the park opens will give you a head start; the queues become very long, very fast. Make your way to the essential rides first before queues begin to dampen your *joie de vivre*. If you like your rides fast and furious, try 'Space Mountain' or 'Indiana Jones and the Temple of Doom'. However, the less stomach-hardened may prefer to camp it up on the Mary Poppins carousel ride. 'Star Tours' provides a simulated space ride with a droid at the wheel, and 'Honey I Shrunk the Audience' is a visual feast of effects-driven wizardry. In July and August, The Main Street Electric Parade sees all the Disney characters walking alongside decorated floats that pump out fairytale sounds. Food must be purchased inside the park and it's not cheap, so if you want to save money eat before you enter. Otherwise, try an American theme restaurant or takeaway snack bars. Stop off at Main Street for your souvenir T-shirts and baseball caps on the way out.

Monet's House

Claude Monet's house and gardens, Giverny | 02 32 51 28 21 | Apr–Oct Tue–Sun 10am–6pm. | RER Vernon Journey time: around 45 minutes | 35F. Shop accepts Mastercard, Visa, American Express.

It was in the grounds of Monet's garden at Giverny that the famous Impressionist painter gained inspiration for much of his work. He lived here until his death in 1926, and the house and gardens have now become a busy tourist attraction. For those people familiar with his watercolours, however, they are a must. Looking down from the Japanese bridge on to the lake below where the water lilies float is like stepping into the painting itself. The gardens are open all year round, but the house, which displays copies of Monet's paintings, closes out of season, so check before setting out from Paris's Gare-St-Lazare to Giverny.

Van Gogh Attic Room

place de la Mairie | 01 34 48 03 03 | daily 10am–6pm Closed 20 Dec–5 Jan | RER A Cergy-Préfecture and bus marked Butry. Journey time: around 50 minutes

Van Gogh used this tiny attic room just outside Paris as a studio, amazingly producing over 60 paintings during his two-month stay here in 1890. Clearly psychologically disturbed, in July of the same year he shot himself dead. He is buried in the nearby cemetery The room is open to the public, along with a short film about his troubled life.

Versailles

Château de Versailles | 01 30 83 78 00 | Château: May–Sept Tue–Sun 9am–6.30pm; Oct–Apr Tue–Sun 9am–5.30pm; 45F, 35F after 3.30pm
Grand Trianon and Petit Trianon: May–Sept daily 12 noon–6.30pm; Oct–April daily 12 noon–5.30pm Gardens 7am–7pm; free admission. Guided tours Oct–Apr Sat & Sun (booking advised: 01 39 24 62 62) | RER C Versailles–Rive Gauche

The Palace at Versailles, built in 1624 as a hunting lodge for King Louis XIV, is a magnificent example of the fairytale palace made real. The two main wings were added in 1678 and took 30 years to complete. In 1682 Louis moved in and rarely set foot in Paris again. Versailles is now one of France's top sights. The 75-m Hall of Mirrors, where the 'Sun King' entertained the country's dignitaries, creates stunning light effects. The Apollo Salon and the Queen's bedroom are also open. The gardens boasts The Grand Trianon, a marble 'palace' where an original pavilion once stood, and the Petit Trianon, a favourite of Marie Antoinette.

Once a girls' boarding house . . .

Checking In

Paris has hotels to suit every walllet, from budget hostels to the infamous Ritz. For gay travellers, the Marais has to be the top choice. The following selection includes many reasonably priced places to stay, although there are also some expensive options for those who just can't manage without their luxury bath towels. The good news is that staying centrally doesn't have to wipe out your bank balance.

The Best Beds

Agora

7 rue de la Cossonnerie, 75001 | 01 42 33 46 02 | ② | Les Halles

Centrally located within walking distance of just about everything, Agora isn't gay but is so convenient that it remains a popular destination for gay boys interested in nightlife. The top floors feature cosy rooms and single beds with skylight views of Paris. The decor is a chaotic mix of family photos and naff souvenirs.

The following price guides have been used for accommodation, per room per night :

① = cheap = under 350F

② = moderate = 350F - 900F

③ = expensive = 900F and over

Familia

11 rue des Ecoles, 75005 | 01 43 54 55 27 | ② | DC, Mastercard, Visa, American Express | Jussieu

A warm welcome awaits one and all at this reasonably priced family hotel on the Left Bank. Each room is individually decorated, including some with impressively beautiful mahogany furniture and murals. The owners are extremely knowledgeable about the area and easy to sideline for an informative chat – useful for first-time visitors. If Familia is fully booked (quite likely in high season), try the Hôtel Minerve, which is just next door. The Minerve is owned by the same family and run to exactly the same high standards.

Hôtel des Batignolles

26–28 rue des Batignolles, 75017
01 43 87 79 40
www.batignolles.com
2 DC, Mastercard, Visa.

Spacious rooms with double-glazing, a TV and a quiet courtyard are the main attractions in this converted ex-boarding house for girls. Today, however, it welcomes everybody. Its location, within easy reach of Montmartre, makes it the perfect visitor's hotel. It is stylish, clean, comfortable and extremely reasonably priced.

Hôtel Beaumarchais

3 rue Oberkampf, 75011
01 53 36 86 86 www.hotelbeaumarchais.com
2 Mastercard, Visa, American Express
République

Modernized by its owner with brightly coloured walls and a courtyard below, Beaumarchais attracts those gay men looking for luxury. A short metro ride from its République location drops you off right in the heart of the Marais. Air conditioning, a lift and wheelchair access add to its appeal. It also has double glazing in all the rooms and a hairdryer for those bad hair days.

Hôtel de la Bretonnerie

22 rue Ste-Croix-de-la-Bretonnerie, 75004
01 48 87 77 63 www.hoteldelabretonnerie.com
2 Hôtel-de-Ville

Furnished almost exclusively with items picked up by the owners at auction while the business is closed in August, this welcoming, family-run hotel on 'gay street' offers clean, simple lodgings at reasonable prices. What more could anyone ask?

Hôtel Central Marais

33 rue Vieille-du-Temple, 75004 01 48 87 56 08 email: hotelcentralmarais @wanadoo.fr 2 breakfast included Mastercard, Visa Hôtel-de-Ville

Located in the heart of the Marais, Le Central remains the only exclusively gay hotel in Paris. Its reputation for friendly service is legendary. Ten rooms over five floors offer up double beds and a great view of the area's main gay street, making it the perfect base for exploring the city. Unfortunately, sharing a bathroom with one other room is unavoidable – en-suites are non-existent. The rooms are basic but comfortable, with breakfast served in a small salon on the first floor right through the morning. When the office is closed, the bar staff remain on hand to give you any help you need. The owner has a good selection of guides, maps and advice. A separate apartment across the street with shower, living room/kitchenette and small balcony offers a degree more privacy.

Exclusively gay

Hôtel St-Merry

78 rue de la Verrerie, 75004 | 01 42 78 14 15 | 3 | Hôtel-de-Ville

This 16th-century former presbytery (which later became a brothel) was once part of the Church of St-Merri next door but today offers a dash of religious theatricality to guests from around the world. Grand bedrooms, stone walls and furniture in keeping with the building's history, including a guest telephone located inside a confessional box, add to its appeal. The rooms might seem expensive, but the hotel's location near the Pompidou Centre makes it a prime and very popular destination. Walking into reception feels like you're taking a leap into a historical set-piece.

Hôtel de la Place des Vosges

12 rue de Birague, 75004 | 01 42 72 60 46 | 2 | DC, Mastercard, Visa, American Express | St-Paul

This former muleteer's house near the place des Vosges offers great views from its top-floor rooms, 24-hour room service as well as elegant decor. It's close to the splendour of this picturesque square and right on the edge of the Marais, which means it's close to the action. The elegance of the reception and breakfast lounge and the comfortable, if simply decorated, rooms make this hotel a pleasant place to plan your day over coffee and a croissant or two.

Party time at the Central

A hotel with religious connections

Hôtel Ritz

15 place Vendôme, 75001
01 43 16 30 30/fax 01 43 16 31 78
www.ritz.com 3 DC, Mastercard, Visa, American Express
Concorde/Opéra

Pure luxury at steep prices, the Ritz is best known these days as the place from which Princess Diana made her fateful last journey in August 1997. Other luminaries from the past who have stayed here include Coco Chanel, Proust and Hemingway. Plush carpeting throughout, perfectly mannered staff, and bulletproof front windows that look out on to place Vendôme leave you in no doubt as to the kind of people it attracts – big names with big wallets.

Terrass Hôtel

12–14 rue Joseph-de-Maistre, 75018
01 46 06 72 85/Fax 01 42 52 29 11
email: terrass@francenet.fr 3 DC, Mastercard, Visa, American Express
Place de Clichy

Situated right on the Butte Montmartre and with fantastic views of the city, this luxurious, stately building has been owned by the same family for four generations. With 101 rooms, a piano bar and roof terrace restaurant, it offers something for everyone. Although it's certainly a large hotel, it manages not to seem too impersonal. A grand buffet breakfast can be had for 75F. All guests are equally welcome, gay or straight.

Putting on the . . .

GRAND HÔTEL JEANNE D'ARC

3 rue de Jarente, 75004
01 48 87 37 31
1
Mastercard, Visa
St-Paul

The rooms are fairly small but this good-value hotel makes an effort, with murals and friendly staff.

GRANDE HÔTEL DU LOIRET

8 rue des Mauvais-Garçons, 75004
01 48 87 77 00
1
Mastercard, Visa
Hôtel-de-Ville

Situated on 'bad boys' street' and recently renovated, gay travellers flock to this popular hotel in the heart of the Marais, near both the Quetzal and Thermik bars.

LES DEGRÉS DE NÔTRE-DAME

10 rue des Grands-Degrés, 75005
01 55 42 88 88; fax 01 40 46 95 34
2 breakfast included
Mastercard, Visa
Maubert-Mutualité

Tucked away within a short walking distance of the Seine, this friendly hotel includes wooden interiors and immaculate rooms.

HÔTEL ACACIAS

20 rue du Temple, 75004
01 48 87 07 70
1
Hôtel-de-Ville

Basic lodgings with friendly staff and a good number of gay visitors.

HÔTEL DE BORDEAUX

24 rue Davy, 75017
01 46 27 19 23
3
Guy Mocquet

This budget apartment complex is popular with gay travellers. Kitchenettes, showers, TVs and phones.

HÔTEL CARON DE BEAUMARCHAIS

12 rue Vieille-du-Temple, 75004
01 42 72 34 12; fax 01 42 72 34 63
www.carondebeaumarchais.com
2
St-Paul

Fairly small but comfortable rooms in this Marais hotel right next to the gay bars of the area. Gilded mirrors and Chinese bathroom tiling give it a classic look, while double-glazing keeps the rooms quiet at night.

HÔTEL CASTEX
5 rue Castex, 75004
01 42 72 31 52; fax 01 42 72 57 91
www.castexhotel.com
1
Mastercard, Visa
Bastille

On the edge of the Marais, this comfortable, good-value hotel has simply decorated rooms, a small salon and smart kitchen (which can also be used by guests). All rooms have a shower/bath and most have a toilet.

HÔTEL DU CYGNE
3 rue du Cygne, 75001
01 42 60 14 16; fax 01 42 21 37 02
2 double; breakfast 40F
Mastercard, Visa
Châtelet

In the heart of Les Halles, this 17th-century mansion offers comfortable, cheap accommodation with wooden beams and antique furniture.

HÔTEL DE LA HERSE D'OR
20 rue St-Antoine, 75004
01 48 87 84 09; fax 01 48 87 94 01 1
breakfast 20F
Bastille

Basic accommodation overlooking the busy rue St-Antoine. Rooms are a good size. Ask for an en-suite bathroom (there aren't many).

HÔTEL LANCASTER
7 rue de Berri, 75008
01 40 76 49 76; fax 01 40 76 40 00
www.hotel-lancaster.fr
3
breakfast 131F
Visa, AmEx
George V

Exquisite town house known for its famous lesbian tenants, Marlene Dietrich and Greta Garbo. Individually designed rooms, a health club, private parking and a smart porter complete the package.

HÔTEL DE LILLE
8 rue du Pélican, 75001
01 42 33 33 42
1
breakfast included
Pont Neuf

Near the Palais Royal. Offers basic, comfortable rooms at low prices. Ask for a room with an ensuite or you'll have to make do with a basin.

HÔTEL LOUXOR
4 rue Taylor, 75009
01 42 08 23 91
2
breakfast 25F
Strasbourg St-Denis

Friendly, good value lodgings, popular with gay visitors. It's about a 20-minute walk from the Marais. Ask the staff for advice on everything from where to eat to the best excursions. Bright, cheery rooms with helpful English-speaking staff.

MARY'S
15 rue de Malte, 75011
01 47 00 81 70
1
Oberkampf

Very cheap and gay friendly, this small, basic hotel is a stone's throw from place de la République. Ideal if you're on a tight budget.

L'Hôtel – Oscar Wilde's last lodgings

HÔTEL MONDIA

22 rue du Grand Prieuré, 75011

01 47 00 93 44

breakfast 35F

Mastercard, Visa, American Express

Overkampf

This two-star gay-friendly hotel, located between Opéra-Garnier and Opéra-Bastille, has 23 recently refurbished rooms and is within easy reach of the Marais and other central locations. Bright, comfortable rooms. Staff speak English.

HÔTEL RÉSIDENCE BOUQUET DE LONGCHAMP

6 rue du Bouquet de Longchamp, 75016

01 47 04 41 71; fax 01 47 27 29 09

breakfast 55F

DC, Mastercard, Visa, American Express

Boissière

Cosy rooms with a peaceful courtyard and pastel interiors. The owner speaks three languages, including English.

HÔTEL SANSONNET

48 rue de la Verrerie, 75004

01 48 87 96 14; fax 01 48 87 30 46

hotelsansonnet@wanadoo.fr

breakfast 40F

DC, Mastercard, Visa, American Express

Hôtel-de-Ville

Wrought-iron staircases and newly renovated rooms signal great changes at this ex-cheap walk-in. The rooms remain simply decorated, but the doubles have en-suite bathrooms, double-glazing, hairdryers and TV.

HÔTEL ST-GERMAIN

88 rue du Bac, 75007

01 49 54 70 00; fax 01 45 48 26 89

breakfast 45F

Mastercard, Visa, American Express

rue du Bac

Moderately priced with 29 rooms, a conservatory, leather sofas and stone walls. Art books and exhibition catalogues available downstairs.

HÔTEL ST-LOUIS MARAIS

1 rue Charles V, 75004

01 48 87 87 04; fax 01 48 87 33 26

www.saintlouismarais.com

breakfast 45F

Mastercard, Visa

Bastille

Decked out with wooden beams and thick carpets, this little slice of Parisian elegance has 16 rooms, double-glazing, hairdryers and TVs.

HÔTEL DU SEPTIÈME ART

20 rue St-Paul, 75004

01 44 54 85 00; fax 01 42 77 69 10

breakfast 45F

DC, Mastercard, Visa, American Express

St-Paul

Smart in a 'pop' kind of way, this 32-bedroomed hotel is decorated with movie memorabilia. Disappointingly, the rooms are more sedate, decked out in beautiful beige. Extremely cheap prices and cool black-and-white-checked floors in the reception areas make it an interesting choice for the first-time traveller.

HÔTEL SCRIBE

1 rue Scribe, 75009

01 44 71 24 24; fax 01

42 65 39 97
scribe@reservation.wanadoo.fr
3
breakfast 110F
Mastercard, Visa, American Express
Opéra

Luxurious living with an artistic edge at this pricey hotel. The Lumière brothers presented the world's first public film projection here and in 1999 artists were invited to design installations in the rooms. The decor is classic Parisian chic.

HÔTEL TIQUETONNE

6 rue Tiquetonne, 75002
01 42 36 94 58; fax 01 42 36 02 94
1
Mastercard, Visa
Etienne-Marcel

Cheap, clean and centrally located just a few steps away from Les Halles, this 47-room hotel offers superb value. All double rooms have an en-suite bathroom; singles aren't all so well equipped. Close to the red-light area of rue St-Denis.

HÔTEL DES TUILERIES

10 rue St-Hyacinthe, 75001
01 42 61 04 17; fax 01 49 27 91 56
www.hotel-des-tuileries.com
2
breakfast 60F
DC, Mastercard, Visa, American Express
Tuileries

Just moments away from the cruisey Tuileries and Tata Beach, this 26-room hotel has a listed

Room with a view

spiral staircase, cellar breakfast room and interior greenhouse in luxurious surroundings. It's very popular and always full so be sure to book ahead.

HÔTEL DE VIGNY

9 rue Balzac, 75008
01 42 99 80 80; fax 01 40 75 05 81 ③
Mastercard, Visa, American Express
George V

High style yet low key, with individually decorated rooms and a tranquil setting near the Champs-Elysées but away from the main tourist area. Air conditioning, TVs and hairdryers in all rooms.

L'HÔTEL

13 rue des Beaux-Arts, 75006
01 44 41 99 00
breakfast 110F
Mastercard, Visa, American Express
St-Germain-des-Prés

Oscar Wilde died in this upmarket fashion palace, which has recently been restored and revamped by the new owner Jean-Paul Besnard. The rooms are expensive, but you get what you pay for.

HOTEL CHAINS

HOLIDAY INN

0800 905999
www.holiday.inn.com
② (prices vary according to location and time of year)
DC, Mastercard, Visa, American Express

American-owned hotel chain with branches across Paris. A wide range of prices and styles is available from basic accommodation to executive suites.

LIBERTEL

01 44 74 17 47
www.libertelhotels.com
②
breakfast 40F
DC, Mastercard, Visa, American Express

Popular chain with a selection of branches, from the very small to the more elaborate.

TIMHÔTEL

01 58 38 37 36
www.timhotel.fr
② 470F single/double; breakfast 50F
DC, Mastercard, Visa, American Express

Popular European chain with indiv-idually decorated rooms and branches across Paris.

HOSTELS

ASSOCIATION DES ÉTUDIANTS PROTESTANTS DE PARIS

46 rue de Vaugirard, 75006
01 46 33 23 30; fax 01 46 34 27 09 (24 hours)
①
breakfast included; membership 10F, paid on arrival; 200F deposit
Mabillon

Dormitories for 18–30s, sharing with eight other people. Price includes kitchen, café and TV room.

BVJ PARIS

44 rue des Bernardins, 75005
01 43 29 34 80; fax 01 53 00 90 91
①
breakfast included
Maubert-Mutualité

Cheap sleeps in a basic but modern environment, with TV lounge. Also at 20 rue Jean-Jacques Rousseau, 75001 (tel: 01 53 00 90).

RESIDENCE LE FAUCONNIER

11 rue du Fauconnier, 75004
01 42 74 23 45 (7am–1am daily).
①
breakfast included

Converted mansion drawing a mixed bag of gay men and other travellers. Early booking is advised.

RESIDENCE MAUBISSON
12 rue des Barres, 75004
01 42 74 23 45
(7am–1am daily).
1
breakfast included
Pont-Marie

Exposed stone, wooden beams and shared accommodation in this popular hostel for budget travellers.

Gay-Advertised Apartments

HOTEL CENTRAL MARAIS ROMANTIC GARDEN STUDIO APARTMENT
6 rue Linné, 75005
www.gayplaces2stay.com
Jussieu

Clean, comfortable studio on the ground floor with flowered courtyard, fully equipped kitchen, microwave and washing machine.

MARAIS HIDE OUT
16 rue Charlemagne, 75004
www.gayplaces2stay.com
St-Paul

Two-bedroomed apartment near the Seine and five minutes from Nôtre Dame and the Louvre. Located on the third floor, it has a peaceful courtyard beneath. Towels, linen and kitchen utensils are also included.

APART-HOTELS
Paris Apartments Services
69 rue d'Argout, 75002
01 40 28 01 28; fax 01 40 28 92 01
www.paris.appartements-services.fr
Mon–Fri 9am–7pm; Sat 10am–noon
3
Studios and apartments from 4,860F per week

A bit pricey, but ideal if you're travelling in a group, this apartment chain has properties throughout central Paris. Included are maid service and 24-hour helpline. English-speaking staff.

SLEEPING AROUND

Gay Stays

Despite the large number of gay visitors, Paris still has only one exclusively gay hotel, the Hôtel Central (see recommended hotels, p. 118). However, many hoteliers either advertise for gay tourists or welcome you whatever your sexuality. The Marais is particularly welcoming to gay guests, and ideal if you want to be close to the gay scene. If you're looking for luxury, you'll pay for it. But some of the more basic lodgings remain good value and have fabulous locations. The following agency and websites specialise in gay-friendly accommodation.

MAN AROUND
89 Wembley Park Drive, Middlesex, England
www.manaround.com
Mon–Fri 9am–6pm, Sat 10am–2pm
Gay specialist travel company providing holidays around the globe.

www.gayplaces2stay.com
Website featuring a list of gay-friendly hotels and a selection of apartments.

www.whatsonwhen.com
Travel information, special events and accommodation for gay people in locations around the world.

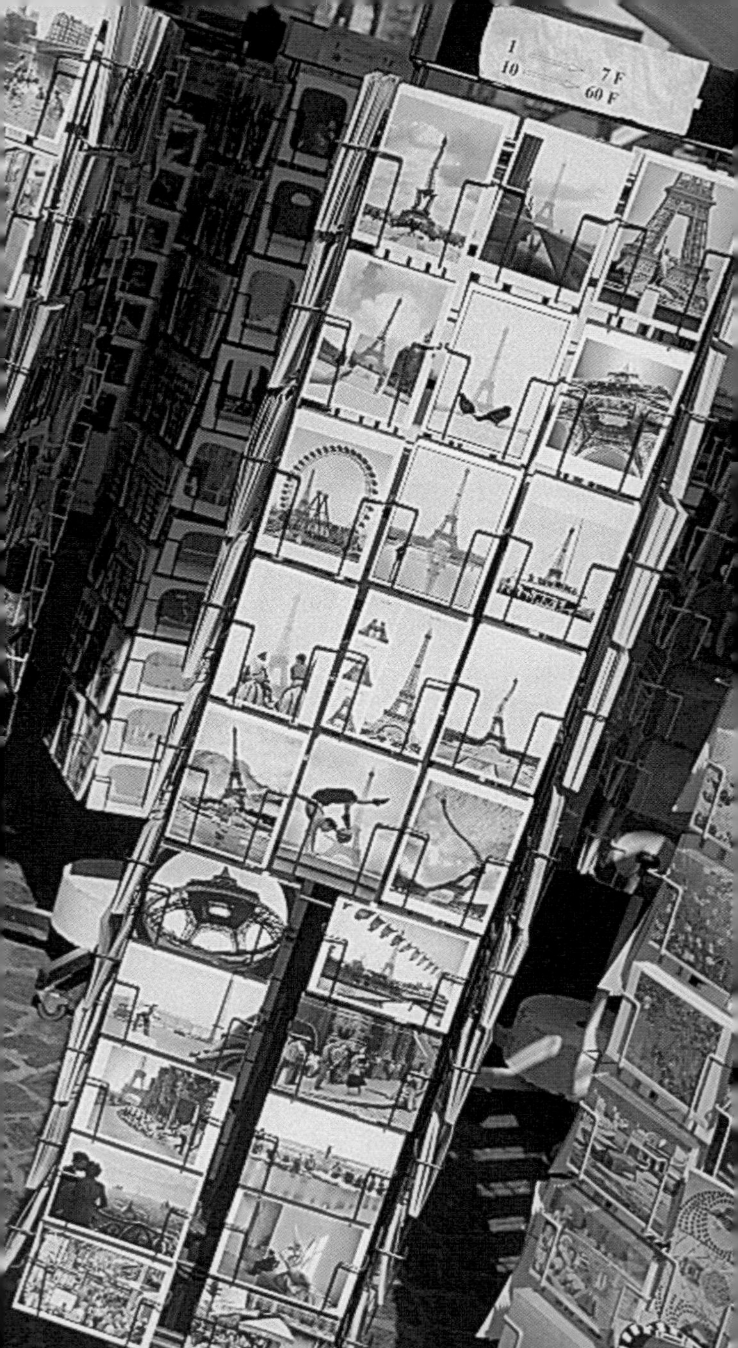

Pick a card . . .

Check This Out

Travelling to Paris from the UK couldn't be easier. The Eurostar train from London's Waterloo station takes around three hours, terminating at Gare du Nord in Paris. From here, you can take the Métro, bus or taxi to your destination. The service leaves London every hour, with some trains stopping at Ashford International and Lille before terminating in Paris. Despite the Eurostar's popularity as a convenient means of transport, arriving by air remains that extra bit special. Don't forget to pack your passport before you leave, and why not use your visit to stock up on French goodies, especially wine.

Getting There

ARRIVING BY AIR

British Airways, Air France and British Midland all fly from various points across the UK to either Orly or Charles de Gaulle airports. Air fares vary enormously, so it pays to shop around. Don't forget to budget for a taxi or train ride when you arrive in France. Neither airport is particularly convenient to get to or from using public transport. If you're on a tight budget, the Air Traffic Advisory Bureau (020-7636 5000) in London has a database crammed with cut-price offers from the UK.

There are direct flights to Paris from over 30 major North American cities and a good selection of airlines to choose from, so tickets are fairly reasonable (around $600). The cheapest is the non-refundable Apex fare, which you must book at least 21 days in advance. Mid-week departures and stay restrictions are the usual rule of thumb. Discounted fares can also be obtained through 'bucket shops', advertised in travel sections of newspapers such as the *LA Times*, *Washington Post* and *New York Times*. Check for hidden extras before purchasing.

Air France is the main airline for non-stop flights from Los Angeles, Miami, Chicago, New York and Washington, DC, but fares are generally more expensive than the American-based airlines. In Canada, Air Canada (www.aircanada.ca) has daily, non-stop flights to Paris from Toronto and Montreal, with connecting flights from Vancouver. All flights are more expensive during the summer.

ROISSY-CHARLES-DE-GAULLE AIRPORT

23km northeast of the city

This is Paris's main airport. British Airways, Air France and most transatlantic flights touch down here. If you land at Terminal 1, take the airport shuttle bus to Roissy's TGV station, where trains run into the city, stopping at Gare du Nord and Châtelet stations. Terminal 2 is closer to Roissy, so walking is a better option. The train from Roissy to Gare du Nord takes about 30 minutes and costs around 55F. A cheaper option is to take the Roissy bus, which leaves every 15 minutes and stops at the Opéra-Garnier, near Opéra Métro station. Air France buses also run every 15 minutes, stopping at avenue Carnot, near the Arc de Triomphe. The journey takes around 45 minutes.

ORLY AIRPORT

14km south of the city

Orly-Rail operates a bus service every 20 minutes from 5.40am–11.15pm; the fare is 40F. This takes you to Pont de Rungis RER station (line C), with trains to Gare d'Austerlitz, Musée d'Orsay and other Métro-linked stations. The journey time is about 35 minutes. Orlyval also has trains running every 7 minutes from 6.30am–10.15pm, arriving at Anthony (RER line B), with connections to Châtelet-Les-Halles. The journey takes about 30 minutes.

Both Orly and Roissy-Charles-de-Gaulle airports have taxi ranks located directly outside the main entrance. Trips are likely to cost you about 200F, depending on your destination. Speak to the driver first if you need a rough price estimate before you depart.

ARRIVING BY RAIL AND BUS

Reaching the city of lights from the UK via rail or bus is far cheaper and less painful than you might think. The train service from London Victoria connects with cross-Channel ferries (yes, they are still operating!) and then continues via rail on reaching France. The journey takes 6–8 hours. Services to Paris also run from a number of other cities across the UK, including Edinburgh, Manchester and Birmingham. Fares are around £50–£60 return.

Gard du Nord

PASSPORTS AND VISAS

If you are travelling from the United Kingdom, America, Australia or Canada, you do not require a visa for a short-term stay of up to 90 days, provided you have a valid passport and are a citizen of the country from which you're travelling. If you are planning to remain in France for longer than 90 days, however, you will need a visa.

Information on requirements can be obtained at: www.diplomatie.gouv.fr/venir/visas/index.gb.html, or www.info-france.org/visa/introduction (for American visitors).

CUSTOMS

Tax must be paid on goods in the country of origin. There are no limits on the quantity of goods taken into France from another EU country, provided tax has been paid on them and they are for personal use. Quantities considered to be for personal use are: up to 800 cigars, 400 cigarellos or 1kg of loose tobacco, 10 litres of spirits (over 22% alcohol), 90 litres of wine (under 22% alcohol) or 110 litres of beer. Amounts considered for personal use from outside the EU are: 200 cigarettes, 50 cigars, 100 cigarellos or 250g of loose tobacco, 1 litre of spirits and 2 litres of beer or wine. You can also carry up to 50,000F in currency.

In the City

TOURIST OFFICES AND INFORMATION

There are several tourist information offices in Paris, providing up-to-the-minute details on accommodation, travel, city tours and entertainment. They also provide some maps and guides free of charge. The main office is at 127 avenue des Champs-Elysées (01 49 52 53 54; open 9am–8pm all year round; Métro Charles de Gaulle-Etoile). There are also smaller centres at main train stations, including Gare du Nord – a handy location if you're arriving by Eurostar. A recorded-information service (in French and English) is also available (01 49 52 53 56) but you are unlikely to need it. Employees manning the information desks are highly knowledgeable about the city and speak a variety of languages, including English.

ACCOMMODATION

For information on places to stay, Paris Travel Service (01992 456000) has a wide range of packages from around £200 per week. All the latest information on accommodation can also be obtained from the French Tourist Office on 0906 824-4123 (60p per minute).

PUBLIC TRANSPORT

METRO AND RER TRAINS

The easiest way to get around Paris is by using the Métro underground train service that links the city stations via a series of numbered lines 1–14. Tickets are available from the windows inside each station but the best option for a short-stay visitor is to purchase a Paris Visite card that allows unlimited travel throughout the city's Métro, bus and RER rail network. The Paris Visite pass, valid for 2, 3 or 5 days and covering zones 1–3, 1–5 or 1–8, can be picked up from any Métro station.

Tickets are generally sold in *carnets* of ten for 52F but can be bought individually for 8F. If you're going out of town, make sure you have the correct ticket. On-the-spot-checks are common and you're unlikely to be treated sympathetically if you don't have a valid pass.

When you have bought your ticket, check the final destination of the train in order to gauge which line and direction you should be travelling. For example, to get to the Bastille from Hôtel-de-Ville Métro, take line 1 towards Château de Vincennes. For Palais-Royal, take line 1 towards La Défense. Some stations also have RER connections, providing an overground service to the suburbs.

To get through the barriers put your ticket through the slot to the side of the gate. When it appears through the top of the machine, retrieve it and walk through the gate. Getting out of the Métro is even easier: simply push the gate and walk through. It's unlikely you'll need help, but if you do, the ticket attendants are usually quite happy to assist you. Many of them also speak English.

Throughout this guide the nearest Métro or RER station has been mentioned. One word of warning: pick pockets operate within the Métro network, so keep all your belongings well hidden. Apart from this, the Métro is safe.

BUS

If you prefer to discover the city above ground, the bus system is reliable and comprehensive. If you have a Paris Visite card, just walk on and put the ticket through the machine. If not, simply buy a ticket from the driver. During the rush hour, between 5pm–7pm, the buses get very busy and can get quite uncomfortable. Day travel is recommended, providing a brighter way to explore the city.

On the buses

From about 1.30am, then at half-hour intervals until 5.30am, the night bus system kicks in; 18 routes depart from the avenue Victoria bus stops in Châtelet at identical times, so all you need to do is match up your stop with the bus routes and hop on board. The driver will only stop on instruction so, if in doubt, ask.

WALKING

Despite the number of Métro stations and bus stops, Paris is easily negotiated on foot. Walking from Hôtel-de-Ville to the Louvre takes around 15 minutes, with plenty of shopping opportunities along the way. From the same point, Nôtre-Dame is just a ten-minute walk and there are plenty of other attractions that seem so near yet so far on the Métro. Take a map and enjoy!

CLIMATE

Despite its 'Continental' feel, Paris's weather remains much the same as in London, although it does fare rather better in the summer months, when temperatures can reach the upper 20s°C (80s°F). The best time to visit the city is during late spring and early autumn, when temperatures are comfortable. During the winter they drop sharply to about 3°C (38°F).

CURRENCY AND BANKS

On 1 January 2002 the official currency of France became the euro, with the value of the euro set at 6.56F. Since that date, the French franc is no longer legal tender.

If you want to change traveller's cheques or cash, the best place to do so is at a bank. These are generally open Mon–Fri from 9am–5pm, closing for two hours at lunchtime. There are many *bureaux de change*, particularly near the centre, but these may have less favourable exchange rates. Commission rates vary, so it's worth shopping around.

EMBASSIES AND CONSULATES

If you get into trouble during your visit, your Embassy or Consulate is there to help you.

US EMBASSY
2 avenue Gabriel, 75006
(33) 1 43 12 22 22

UK EMBASSY
18 bis rue d'Anjou, 75008
01 44 51 31 02
www.arnb-grandebretagne.fr/consularservices

AUSTRALIAN EMBASSY
4 rue Jean-Rey, 75724
01 40 59 33 00
www.austgov.fr

CANADIAN EMBASSY
35 avenue Montaigne, 75008
(33-1) 44 43 29 00
www.amb-canada.fr

POLICE AND CRIME

Paris remains a fairly safe city, but the number of pickpockets and other scam artists in the Métro, particularly in the busy Les Halles district, serve as a reminder to keep your belongings safe at all times. The stranger who comes out of nowhere and bumps into you might have known exactly where they were going, so be careful. If you are the victim of a crime, you should head for the Commissariat

Bureau de Change

de Police of the *arrondissement* in which the crime took place. The first thing they will do is ask for your passport, before filling out a report of the incident. Although they can be extremely uncooperative, the police are required to assist you. Even if they don't offer you basic courteousness, politeness is always your best option. If you are stopped and asked for your passport, you would be unwise to be difficult or argumentative. The police have a well-deserved reputation for being bullish and sometimes violent.

Their attitude towards homosexuality is also not particularly positive, so don't expect any sympathy if you've been attacked while out cruising. If you're caught carrying or taking illegal drugs, they will arrest you and you could end up in prison. No matter what your nationality, your embassy will not be able to help you if you violate French law. A list of English-speaking lawyers in Paris may be the only assistance they can provide if you decide to contact them.

SAFETY AND SECURITY

Paris is generally a safe place to visit, with night-time excursions generally causing few hassles. It is always wise to remain within populated areas and keep your eyes and ears open for trouble. The Métro runs until 1.30am and is a safe mode of transport. The night buses also offer a convenient way of getting home from night clubs (see p. 134).

Explorations of the gay cruising areas around Gare d'Austerlitz and the infamous Port area are ill-advised. You risk being robbed of your passport or even more. The infamous Bois de Boulogne, known for its high levels of trans-sexual prostitutes, is also extremely dangerous at night. An attack in any of these locales is unlikely to get a favourable police response.

HEALTH

It's wise to take out health insurance before you travel, in case you're taken ill during your stay. Citizens of the EU should pick up form E111 from their post office, fill it in and get it stamped. North American and all other non-EU citizens will need private insurance. In the UK most insurance policies require the cost of treatment be paid by the policy holder before being reimbursed. If you plan to drive while on holiday, check that the policy covers you in case of a traffic accident.

If you are the victim of a crime, you must report it to the police in order to claim on any policy. You should also check your house contents insurance to see if your credit cards are included. And

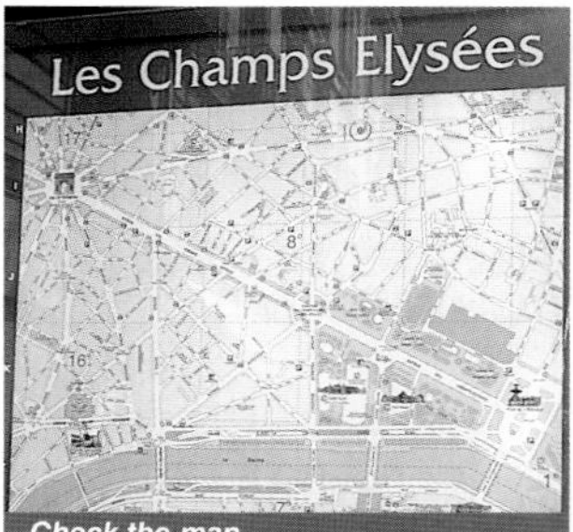

Check the map . . .

. . follow the signs

always read the small print on any document. No vaccinations are required before entering France.

PHARMACIES

Highly visible due to their large, green cross above the door, pharmacies are plentiful across Paris. Some open late into the evening or for 24 hours. Among these are:

PHARMACIE DES HALLES

10 boulevard de Sébastopol, 75004
01 42 72 03 23
Mon–Sat 9am–midnight; Sun 9am–10pm | Châtelet

PHARMACIE DES CHAMPS

84 avenue des Champs-Elysées, 75008 | 01 45 62 02 41
24 hours | George .

PHARMACIE DU VILLAGE

26 rue de Temple, 75004
01 42 72 60 71
Hôtel-de-Ville
daily 8.30am–10pm

This pharmacy has a good knowledge of HIV drugs.

HIV AND SAFE SEX

If you're HIV positive, Paris is not the place to run out of medicine. Although most HIV drugs are available internationally, they may have different brand names in France, and be hard to come by. In addition, they cannot be obtained without a prescription, for which you will have to see a French doctor. This may be very time consuming and frustrating. The French embassy suggests you take an ample supply before travelling, along with proof stating that the drugs are for personal use and also what they have been prescribed for, to prevent any unnecessary interest from overzealous customs officers.

If you need advice while in France, you can phone English-speaking HIV/AIDS helpline FACTS on 01 44 93 16 69 or SIDA (AIDS) 24-hour information service on 08 00 84 08 00. A list of gay doctors can be obtained from the Association des Médicins Gais on 01 48 05 81 72.

GAY GROUPS AND RESOURCES

If you're looking for some gay company in Paris, you don't have to look too far. Whatever you're interested in, there's probably a gay group for it. For the short-stay visitor, head down to the Centre Gai et Lesbienne at 3 rue Keller in the Bastille (01 43 57 21 47), Métro Ledru-Rollin. It's open Mon–Sat from 2pm–8pm. Here you'll find all the latest information on social and sporting groups throughout the city, in addition to legal and other services. Free gay magazine *em@le* also has up-to-date listings of activity groups.

GAY LIFE IN THE CITY

Paris has one of the most liberal attitudes in Europe towards gay sex. When President Mitterrand came to power, the age of consent was reduced to 15. Since then, bars and saunas have been testing boundaries daily in their efforts to redefine what is considered off-limits. Public sex remains illegal. During the summer, the infamous Tata beach, between Pont Royal and Pont du Carousel on the banks of the Seine, attracts a lithe-limbed gay crowd.

GAY PRESS

If you're interested in the gay scene, there is a good selection of free magazines to be found in bars, clubs and gay cafés. If you're looking for something more general, the best listings guide for the arts, entertainments and restaurants is *Paris Scope* (3F), available at news-stands every Wednesday. Fortunately, it also has an English section. *Télerama* (3F) has a listings insert, in addition to features on the arts in French, as does *Officiel des Spectacles* (2F). The French national newspaper *Le Monde* also publishes a weekly listings insert, called *Aden*, every Wednesday.

TELEVISION AND RADIO

There are six main television channels but American imports such as Ally McBeal remain the most popular. A range of satellite channels and two state channels comprise a mix of films, game shows and drama.

Gay publications

COMMUNICATIONS

Public telephones can be found all over the city and they're easy to use, providing you know the dialling code beforehand (the operator is unlikely to speak English). Most call boxes take phone cards (*télécartes*), available in units of 50 and 120. You can purchase them at any post office and many tobacconist (*tabac*) stores. As the French adore their Gauloises, you shouldn't have a problem finding what you're looking for. *Tabacs* are everywhere and identifiable by a red sign above the entrance. Thomas Cook also has an International Telephone Card that uses a PIN code system, costing 50F or 100F. These are available through Thomas Cook agencies (01 47 58 21 00). For local cyber cafés, see Shopping, p74.

The postal system in France can be slow and bureaucratic, but the installation of automatic machines that can weigh your mail and provide the correct stamps have kept queues down. You can also purchase stamps at any tobacconist, along with your *télécarte*.

TELEPHONING

To use public telephones, pick up the receiver and insert your telephone card after the 'Introduisez Votre Carte' prompt. When the screen says 'Numérotez', dial the number, including the dialling code. If you are calling the UK, add 00 44 to the start of the number (dropping the first 0 of the UK dialling code); for the US and Canada add 00 1 and Australia 00 61 respectively. If you want to use a mobile, you should check with your dealer before travelling. Roaming rates can be pricey.

ATMs (AUTOMATIC TELLER MACHINES)

ATMs can be found outside banks and in some post offices. These often have instructions in English.

OPENING HOURS

Opening hours vary enormously in Paris, depending on where you are going. Most shops and museums are open Mon–Sat, and close either on Sundays or Mondays, or both. Some shops also close at lunchtime from about 1–2.30pm.

PUBLIC HOLIDAYS AND FESTIVALS

If you're visiting Paris in August, many shops, museums and restaurants will be closed for the holiday season, so check before travelling if you have a particular place you want to visit. Hotels are open all year round and some have discounts during the quieter months. If you're looking for a party, Gay Pride takes place in late June each year, when brightly coloured floats, parades and a festival take over the city in a celebration of pink Paree. Look on the internet at www.gaypride.fr, or contact the Centre Gai et Lesbienne (see Gay Groups and Resources, p. 138) for more information.

TIME

Paris runs on the 24-hour clock, so 1pm would be 1300 hrs and 12 midnight 2400 hrs. The city is one hour ahead of Greenwich Mean Time (GMT) and six hours ahead of Eastern Seaboard Time.

ELECTRICITY

Electricity in France runs on 220V, so visitors from the UK will need an adaptor. These can be purchased at most department and electrical stores in teh UK. Visitors from the US, Canada and Australia require a transformer, which may also be bought before travelling or at the BHV department store (see Shopping, p. 74).

TIPPING

All cafés, bars and restaurants include a service charge, which is added to the final bill. However, it is considered extremely impolite not to leave something for the waiter. The amount you give is up to you, but a recommendation is to set aside around 5F for a coffee and 50F for an average-priced meal. This will ensure the waiter makes a special effort.

Kiss me quick

INDEX

INDEX

NOTEBOOK

NOTEBOOK

NOTEBOOK

NOTEBOOK

NOTEBOOK

CONTACT LIST

Name
Address

Tel
Fax
email

Name
Address

Tel
Fax
email

Name
Address

Tel
Fax
email

Name
Address

Tel
Fax
email

Name
Address

Tel
Fax
email

Name
Address

Tel
Fax
email

CONTACT LIST

Name

Address

Tel

Fax

email

Name

Address

Tel

Fax

email

Name

Address

Tel

Fax

email

Name

Address

Tel

Fax

email

Name

Address

Tel

Fax

email

Name

Address

Tel

Fax

email

CONTACT LIST

Name

Address

Tel

Fax

email

Name

Address

Tel

Fax

email

Name

Address

Tel

Fax

email

Name

Address

Tel

Fax

email

Name

Address

Tel

Fax

email

Name

Address

Tel

Fax

email

Fill in details of your favourite restaurants below . . .
Tell us about them by logging on to www.outaround.com

Restaurant

Contact Details

Comments

Restaurant

Contact Details

Comments

Restaurant

Contact Details

Comments

My Top Restaurants

My Top Bars

Fill in details of your favourite bars below . . .
Tell us about them by logging on to www.outaround.com

Bar

Contact Details

Comments

Bar

Contact Details

Comments

Bar

Contact Details

Comments

Fill in details of your favourite clubs below . . .
Tell us about them by logging on to www.outaround.com

Club

Contact Details

Comments

Club

Contact Details

Comments

Club

Contact Details

Comments

My Top Clubs

Feedback Form

If you enjoyed using this book, or even if you didn't, please help us improve future editions by taking part in our reader survey. Every returned form will be acknowledged and to show our appreciation we will send you a voucher entitling you to £1 off your next Out Around guide or any other Thomas Cook guidebook. Just take a few minutes to complete and return this form to us.

Alternatively you can visit www.outaround.com and email us the answers to the questions using the numbers given below.

We'd also be glad to hear of your comments, updates or recommendations on places we cover or you think that we ought to cover.

1 Which Out Around guide did you purchase?

2 Have you purchased other Out Around guides in the series?

☐ Yes ☐ No If Yes, please specify

3 Which of the following tempted you into buying your Out Around guide. (Please tick as appropriate)

☐ The price
☐ The rainbow spine
☐ The cover
☐ The fact it was a dedicated gay travel guide
☐ Other

4 Please rate the following features of your 'Out Around guide' for their value to you (circle VU for 'very useful', U for 'useful', NU for 'little or no use')

'A Day Out' features	VU	U	NU
Top Sights	VU	U	NU
Top restaurants and cafés and listings	VU	U	NU
Top shops and listings	VU	U	NU
Top hotels and listings	VU	U	NU
Top clubs and bars and listings	VU	U	NU
Theatre and music venues	VU	U	NU
Gyms and sauna choices	VU	U	NU
Practical information	VU	U	NU

Feedback Form

5 How did you book your holiday?

- ☐ Package deal
- ☐ Package deal through a gay-specific tour operator
- ☐ Flight only
- ☐ Accommodation only
- ☐ Flight and accommodation booked separately

6 How many people are travelling in your party?

7 Which other cities do you intend to/have travelled to in the next/past 12 months?

Amsterdam	Yes ☐	No ☐
London	Yes ☐	No ☐
Miami	Yes ☐	No ☐
New York	Yes ☐	No ☐
Paris	Yes ☐	No ☐
San Francisco	Yes ☐	No ☐

Other (please specify)

8 Please use this space to tell us about any features that in your opinion could be changed, improved, or added in future editions of the book, or any other comments you would like to make concerning the book:

9 Your age category
☐ under 21 ☐ 21-30 ☐ 31-40 ☐ 41-50 ☐ 51+

First name (or initials)

Last name

Your full address (Please include postal or zip code)

Your daytime telephone number:

From time to time we send our readers details of new titles or special offers. Please tick here if you wish your name to be held on our mailing list (Note: our mailing list is never sold to other companies). ☐

Please detach this page and send it to: The Editor, Out Around, Thomas Cook Publishing, PO Box 227, The Thomas Cook Business Park, Peterborough PE3 8XX, United Kingdom.